Pope, Gray, Goldsmith; Selected Poems;
Essay on Criticism, Elegy Written in a
Country Churchyard, The Progress of Poesy,
The Traveller, The Deserted Village

𝔗𝔥𝔢 𝔄𝔠𝔞𝔡𝔢𝔪𝔶 𝔖𝔢𝔯𝔦𝔢𝔰 𝔬𝔣 𝔈𝔫𝔤𝔩𝔦𝔰𝔥 ℭ𝔩𝔞𝔰𝔰𝔦𝔠𝔰

POPE, GRAY, GOLDSMITH

SELECTED POEMS

ESSAY ON CRITICISM
ELEGY WRITTEN IN A COUNTRY CHURCHYARD
THE PROGRESS OF POESY
THE TRAVELLER
THE DESERTED VILLAGE

EDITED BY

GEORGE A. WATROUS, A.M.
UTICA FREE ACADEMY, UTICA, NEW YORK

ALLYN AND BACON

𝔅𝔬𝔰𝔱𝔬𝔫 𝔞𝔫𝔡 ℭ𝔥𝔦𝔠𝔞𝔤𝔬

PREFACE.

THE poems in this volume of the *Academy Series* are chosen for the third year of an academy course. All except *The Progress of Poesy* and *The Traveller* are prescribed in the New York State Regents' course. It is believed that the added poems will materially assist the student to a fuller sympathy with the spirit of the respective authors and to a clearer comprehension of their time. *The Traveller* and *The Deserted Village* are certainly companion poems and should be studied together. The *Elegy,* with all its simplicity and beauty, does not represent Gray, for it merely indicates a change of attitude which appears fully developed in *The Progress of Poesy.* The nature of the poems and the relation of the authors to the development of our literature make possible the compilation here offered. The student, it is hoped, may be helped by having in this small compass the five chief poems of the eighteenth century.

G. A. W.

UTICA, N.Y.,
May, 1899.

iii

CONTENTS.

ALEXANDER POPE.

AN ESSAY ON CRITICISM.

AN ESSAY ON CRITICISM.

I.

Introduction : — That 'tis as great a fault to judge ill as to write ill, and a more dangerous one to the public, v. 1.   That a true taste is as rare to be found as a true genius, vv. 9 to 18.   That most men are born with some taste, but spoiled by false education, vv. 19 to 25.

The multitude of critics, and causes of them, vv. 26 to 45.   That we are to study our own taste, and know the limits of it, vv. 46 to 67.

Nature the best guide of judgment, vv. 68 to 87.   Improved by art and rules, which are but methodized nature, v. 88.

Rules derived from the practice of the ancient poets, vv. 1d to 110. That therefore the ancients are necessary to be studied, by a critic, particularly Homer and Virgil, vv. 120 to 138.

Of licenses, and the use of them by the ancients, vv. 140 to 180. Reverence due to the ancients, and praise of them, vv. 181, etc.

'Tis hard to say, if greater want of skill
Appear in writing or in judging ill;
But, of the two, less dangerous is the offence
To tire our patience, than mislead our sense.
Some few in that, but numbers err in this,   5
Ten censure wrong for one who writes amiss;
A fool might once himself alone expose,
Now one in verse makes many more in prose.
　　'Tis with our judgments as our watches, none
Go just alike, yet each believes his own.   10

3

In poets as true genius is but rare,
True taste as seldom is the critic's share;
Both must alike from Heaven derive their light,
These born to judge, as well as those to write.
Let such teach others who themselves excel, 15
And censure freely who have written well.
Authors are partial to their wit, 'tis true,
But are not critics to their judgment, too?
   Yet if we look more closely, we shall find
Most have the seeds of judgment in their mind: 20
Nature affords at least a glimmering light;
The lines, though touched but faintly, are drawn right.
But as the slightest sketch, if justly traced,
Is by ill-coloring but the more disgraced,
So by false learning is good sense defaced: 25
Some are bewildered in the maze of schools,
And some made coxcombs nature meant but fools.
In search of wit these lose their common sense,
And then turn critics in their own defence:
Each burns alike, who can, or cannot write, 30
Or with a rival's, or an eunuch's spite.
All fools have still an itching to deride,
And fain would be upon the laughing side.
If Mævius scribble in Apollo's spite,
There are who judge still worse than he can write. 35
   Some have at first for wits, then poets, past,
Turned critics next, and proved plain fools at last.
Some neither can for wits nor critics pass,
As heavy mules are neither horse nor ass.
Those half-learned witlings, numerous in our isle, 40
As half-formed insects on the banks of Nile;
Unfinished things, one knows not what to call,
Their generation's so equivocal:

To tell 'em, would a hundred tongues require,
Or one vain wit's, that might a hundred tire.   45
   But you who seek to give and merit fame,
And justly bear a critic's noble name,
Be sure yourself and your own reach to know,
How far your genius, taste, and learning go;
Launch not beyond your depth, but be discreet,   50
And mark that point where sense and dulness meet.
   Nature to all things fixed the limit fit,
And wisely curbed proud man's pretending wit.
As on the land while here the ocean gains,
In other parts it leaves wide sandy plains;   55
Thus in the soul while memory prevails,
The solid power of understanding fails;
Where beams of warm imagination play,
The memory's soft figures melt away.
One science only will one genius fit;   60
So vast is art, so narrow human wit:
Not only bounded to peculiar arts,
But oft in those confined to single parts.
Like kings we lose the conquests gained before,
By vain ambition still to make them more;   65
Each might his several province well command,
Would all but stoop to what they understand.
   First follow nature, and your judgment frame
By her just standard, which is still the same:
Unerring nature, still divinely bright,   70
One clear, unchanged, and universal light,
Life, force, and beauty, must to all impart,
At once the source, and end, and test of art.
Art from that fund each just supply provides,
Works without show, and without pomp presides: 75
In some fair body thus the informing soul

With spirits feeds, with vigor fills the whole,
Each motion guides, and every nerve sustains;
Itself unseen, but in the effects, remains.
Some, to whom Heaven in wit has been profuse,   80
Want as much more, to turn it to its use;
For wit and judgment often are at strife,
Though meant each other's aid, like man and wife.
'Tis more to guide, than spur the Muse's steed;
Restrain his fury, then provoke his speed;   85
The winged courser, like a generous horse,
Shows most true metal when you check his course.
   Those rules of old discovered, not devised,
Are nature still, but nature methodized;
Nature, like liberty, is but restrained   90
By the same laws which first herself ordained.
   Hear how learned Greece her useful rules indites,
When to repress, and when indulge our flights:
High on Parnassus' top her sons she showed,
And pointed out those arduous paths they trod;   95
Held from afar, aloft, the immortal prize,
And urged the rest by equal steps to rise.
Just precepts thus from great examples given,
She drew from them what they derived from Heaven.
The generous critic fanned the poet's fire,   100
And taught the world with reason to admire.
Then Criticism the Muse's handmaid proved,
To dress her charms, and make her more beloved:
But following wits from that intention strayed,
Who could not win the mistress, wooed the maid;   105
Against the poets their own arms they turned,
Sure to hate most the men from whom they learned.
So modern 'pothecaries, taught the art
By doctor's bills to play the doctor's part,

Bold in the practice of mistaken rules,   . 110
Prescribe, apply, and call their masters fools.
Some on the leaves of ancient authors prey,
Nor time nor moths e'er spoiled so much as they.
Some dryly plain, without invention's aid,
Write dull receipts how poems may be made.   115
These leave the sense, their learning to display,
And those explain the meaning quite away.
     You then whose judgment the right course would steer,
Know well each ancient's proper character;
His fable, subject, scope in every page;   120
Religion, country, genius of his age:
Without all these at once before your eyes,
Cavil you may, but never criticise.
Be Homer's works your study and delight,
Read them by day, and meditate by night;   125
Thence form your judgment, thence your maxims bring,
And trace the Muses upward to their spring.
Still with itself compared, his text peruse;
And let your comment be the Mantuan Muse.
     When first young Maro in his boundless mind   130
A work to outlast immortal Rome designed,
Perhaps he seemed above the critic's law,
And but from nature's fountains scorned to draw:
But when to examine every part he came,
Nature and Homer were, he found, the same.   135
Convinced, amazed, he checks the bold design;
And rules as strict his labored work confine,
As if the Stagirite o'erlooked each line.
Learn hence for ancient rules a just esteem;
To copy nature is to copy them.   140
     Some beauties yet no precepts can declare,
For there's a happiness as well as care.

Music resembles poetry, in each
Are nameless graces which no methods teach,
And which a master-hand alone can reach.   145
If, where the rules not far enough extend
(Since rules were made but to promote their end),
Some lucky license answer to the full
The intent proposed, that license is a rule.
Thus Pegasus, a nearer way to take,   150
May boldly deviate from the common track;
From vulgar bounds with brave disorder part,
And snatch a grace beyond the reach of art,
Which, without passing through the judgment, gains
The heart, and all its end at once attains.   155
In prospects thus, some objects please our eyes,
Which out of nature's common order rise,
The shapeless rock, or hanging precipice.
Great wits sometimes may gloriously offend,
And rise to faults true critics dare not mend.   160
But though the ancients thus their rules invade
(As kings dispense with laws themselves have made),
Moderns, beware! or if you must offend
Against the precept, ne'er transgress its end;
Let it be seldom, and compelled by need;   165
And have, at least, their precedent to plead.
The critic else proceeds without remorse,
Seizes your fame, and puts his laws in force.
  I know they are, to whose presumptuous thoughts
Those freer beauties, ev'n in them, seem faults. 170
Some figures monstrous and mis-shaped appear,
Considered singly, or beheld too near,
Which, but proportioned to their light, or place,
Due distance reconciles to form and grace.
A prudent chief not always must display   175

His powers in equal ranks, and fair array.
But with the occasion and the place comply,
Conceal his force, nay, seem sometimes to fly.
Those oft are stratagems which error seem,
Nor is it Homer nods, but we that dream.   180
   Still green with bays each ancient altar stands,
Above the reach of sacrilegious hands;
Secure from flames, from envy's fiercer rage,
Destructive war, and all-involving age.
See, from each clime the learned their incense bring!   185
Hear, in all tongues consenting pæans ring!
In praise so just let every voice be joined,
And fill the general chorus of mankind.
Hail, bards triumphant! born in happier days;
Immortal heirs of universal praise!   190
Whose honors with increase of ages grow,
As streams roll down, enlarging as they flow;
Nations unborn your mighty names shall sound,
And worlds applaud that must not yet be found!
Oh, may some spark of your celestial fire,   195
The last, the meanest of your sons inspire,
(That on weak wings, from far, pursues your flights,
Glows while he reads, but trembles as he writes),
To teach vain wits a science little known,
To admire superior sense, and doubt their own!   200

II.

Causes hindering a true judgment. 1. Pride, v. 208.   2. Imperfect learning, v. 215.   3. Judging by parts, and not by the whole, vv. 233 to 288. Critics in wit, language, versification only, vv. 288, 305, 339, etc.   4. Being too hard to please, or too apt to admire, v. 384.   5. Partiality — too much love to a sect — to the ancients or moderns, v. 394.   6. Prejudice or prevention, v. 408.   7. Singu-

larity, v. 424.   8. Inconstancy, v. 430.   9. Party spirit, vv. 452,
etc.   10. Envy, v 466   Against envy, and in praise of good
nature, vv. 508, etc.   When severity is chiefly to be used by critics,
vv. 526, etc.

Of all the causes which conspire to blind
Man's erring judgment, and misguide the mind,
What the weak head with strongest bias rules,
Is pride, the never-failing voice of fools.
Whatever nature has in worth denied,   205
She gives in large recruits of needful pride;
For as in bodies, thus in souls, we find
What wants in blood and spirits, swelled with wind:
Pride, where wit fails, steps in to our defence,
And fills up all the mighty void of sense.   210
If once right reason drives that cloud away,
Truth breaks upon us with resistless day.
Trust not yourself; but your defects to know,
Make use of every friend — and every foe.

A *little learning* is a dangerous thing;   215
Drink deep, or taste not the Pierian spring:
There shallow draughts intoxicate the brain,
And drinking largely sobers us again.
Fired at first sight with what the muse imparts,
In fearless youth we tempt the heights of arts,   220
While from the bounded level of our mind
Short views we take, nor see the lengths behind;
But more advanced, behold with strange surprise
New distant scenes of endless science rise!
So pleased at first the towering Alps we try,   225
Mount o'er the vales, and seem to tread the sky,
The eternal snows appear already past,
And the first clouds and mountains seem the last;
But, those attained, we tremble to survey

The growing labors of the lengthened way, 230
The increasing prospect tires our wandering eyes,
Hills peep o'er hills, and Alps on Alps arise!
A perfect judge will read each work of wit
With the same spirit that its author writ:
Survey the whole, nor seek slight faults to find 235
Where nature moves, and rapture warms the mind;
Nor lose, for that malignant dull delight,
The generous pleasure to be charmed with wit.
But in such lays as neither ebb, nor flow,
Correctly cold, and regularly low, 240
That shunning faults, one quiet tenor keep;
We cannot blame indeed — but we may sleep.
In wit, as nature, what affects our hearts
Is not the exactness of peculiar parts;
'Tis not a lip, or eye, we beauty call, 245
But the joint force and full result of all.
Thus when we view some well-proportioned dome
(The world's just wonder, and even thine, O Rome!),
No single parts unequally surprise,
All comes united to the admiring eyes; 250
No monstrous height, or breadth, or length appear;
The whole at once is bold, and regular.
Whoever thinks a faultless piece to see,
Thinks what ne'er was, nor is, nor e'er shall be.
In every work regard the writer's end, 255
Since none can compass more than they intend;
And if the means be just, the conduct true,
Applause, in spite of trivial faults, is due;
As men of breeding, sometimes men of wit,
To avoid great errors, must the less commit: 260
Neglect the rules each verbal critic lays,
For not to know some trifles is a praise.

Most critics, fond of some subservient art,
Still make the whole depend upon a part:
They talk of principles, but notions prize,   265
And all to one loved folly sacrifice.
    Once on a time, La Mancha's knight, they say,
A certain bard encountering on the way,
Discoursed in terms as just, with looks as sage,
As e'er could Dennis of the Grecian stage;   270
Concluding all were desperate sots and fools,
Who durst depart from Aristotle's rules.
Our author, happy in a judge so nice,
Produced his play, and begged the knight's advice;
Made him observe the subject, and the plot,   275
The manners, passions, unities; what not?
All which, exact to rule, were brought about,
Were but a combat in the lists left out
"What! leave the combat out?" exclaims the knight;
Yes, or we must renounce the Stagirite   280
"Not so, by Heaven!" (he answers in a rage),
"Knights, squires, and steeds, must enter on the stage."
So vast a throng the stage can ne'er contain.
"Then build a new, or act it in a plain."
    Thus critics, of less judgment than caprice,   285
Curious not knowing, not exact but nice,
Form short ideas; and offend in arts
(As most in manners) by a love to parts.
    Some to conceit alone their taste confine,
And glittering thoughts struck out at every line;   290
Pleased with a work where nothing's just or fit,
One glaring chaos and wild heap of wit.
Poets like painters, thus, unskilled to trace
The naked nature and the living grace,
With gold and jewels cover every part,   295

And hide with ornaments their want of art.
True wit is nature to advantage dressed,
What oft was thought, but ne'er so well expressed;
Something, whose truth convinced at sight we find,
That gives us back the image of our mind.   300
As shades more sweetly recommend the light,
So modest plainness sets off sprightly wit.
For works may have more wit than does 'em good,
As bodies perish through excess of blood.
    Others for language all their care express,   305
And value books, as women men, for dress:
Their praise is still, — the style is excellent:
The sense, they humbly take upon content.
Words are like leaves; and where they most abound,
Much fruit of sense beneath is rarely found,   310
False eloquence, like the prismatic glass,
Its gaudy colors spreads on every place;
The face of nature we no more survey,
All glares alike, without distinction gay:
But true expression, like the unchanging sun,   315
Clears and improves whate'er it shines upon,
It gilds all objects but it alters none.
Expression is the dress of thought, and still
Appears more decent, as more suitable;
A vile conceit in pompous words expressed   320
Is like a clown in regal purple dressed:
For different styles with different subjects sort,
As several garbs with country, town, and court.
Some by old words to fame have made pretence,
Ancients in phrase, mere moderns in their sense;   325
Such labored nothings, in so strange a style,
Amaze the unlearned, and make the learned smile.
Unlucky, as Fungoso in the play,

These sparks with awkward vanity display
What the fine gentleman wore yesterday; 330
And but so mimic ancient wits at best,
As apes our grandsires, in their doublets dressed.
In words, as fashions, the same rule will hold;
Alike fantastic, if too new, or old:
Be not the first by whom the new are tried, 335
Nor yet the last to lay the old aside.
 But most by numbers judge a poet's song;
And smooth or rough, with them is right or wrong:
In the bright Muse though thousand charms conspire,
Her voice is all these tuneful fools admire; 340
Who haunt Parnassus but to please their ear,
Not mend their minds; as some to church repair,
Not for the doctrine, but the music there.
These equal syllables alone require,
Though oft the ear the open vowels tire; 345
While expletives their feeble aid do join;
And ten low words oft creep in one dull line:
While they ring round the same unvaried chimes,
With sure returns of still expected rhymes;
Where'er you find "the cooling western breeze," 350
In the next line, it "whispers through the trees":
If crystal streams "with pleasing murmurs creep,"
The reader's threatened (not in vain) with "sleep":
Then, at the last and only couplet fraught
With some unmeaning thing they call a thought, 355
A needless Alexandrine ends the song
That, like a wounded snake, drags its slow length along.
Leave such to tune their own dull rhymes, and know
What's roundly smooth or languishingly slow;
And praise the easy vigor of a line, 360
Where Denham's strength, and Waller's sweetness join.

True ease in writing comes from art, not chance,
As those move easiest who have learned to dance.
'Tis not enough no harshness gives offence,
The sound must seem an echo to the sense: 365
Soft is the strain when zephyr gently blows,
And the smooth stream in smoother numbers flows;
But when loud surges lash the sounding shore,
The hoarse, rough verse should like the torrent roar:
When Ajax strives some rock's vast strength to throw, 370
The line, too, labors, and the words move slow;
Not so, when swift Camilla scours the plain,
Flies o'er the unbending corn, and skims along the main.
Hear how Timotheus' varied lays surprise,
And bid alternate passions fall and rise!   375
While, at each change, the son of Libyan Jove
Now burns with glory, and then melts with love,
Now his fierce eyes with sparkling fury glow,
Now sighs steal out, and tears begin to flow:
Persians and Greeks like turns of nature found,   380
And the world's victor stood subdued by sound!
The power of music all our hearts allow,
And what Timotheus was, is Dryden now.

   Avoid extremes; and shun the fault of such,
Who still are pleased too little or too much.   385
At every trifle scorn to take offence,
That always shows great pride or little sense;
Those heads, as stomachs, are not sure the best,
Which nauseate all, and nothing can digest.
Yet let not each gay turn thy rapture move;   390
For fools admire, but men of sense approve:
As things seem large which we through mists descry,
Dulness is ever apt to magnify.

   Some foreign writers, some our own despise;

The ancients only, or the moderns, prize.   395
Thus wit, like faith, by each man is applied
To one small sect, and all are damned beside.
Meanly they seek the blessing to confine,
And force that sun but on a part to shine,
Which not alone the southern wit sublimes,   400
But ripens spirits in cold northern climes;
Which from the first has shone on ages past,
Enlights the present, and shall warm the last;
Though each may feel increases and decays,
And see now clearer and now darker days.   405
Regard not then if wit be old or new,
But blame the false, and value still the true.
    Some ne'er advance a judgment of their own,
But catch the spreading notion of the town;
They reason and conclude by precedent,   410
And own stale nonsense which they ne'er invent.
Some judge of authors' names, not works, and then
Nor praise nor blame the writings, but the men.
Of all this servile herd the worst is he
That in proud dulness joins with quality,   415
A constant critic at the great man's board,
To fetch and carry nonsense for my lord.
What woful stuff this madrigal would be,
In some starved hackney sonneteer, or me?
But let a lord once own the happy lines,   420
How the wit brightens! how the style refines!
Before his sacred name flies every fault,
And each exalted stanza teems with thought!
    The vulgar thus through imitation err;
As oft the learned by being singular;   425
So much they scorn the crowd, that if the throng
By chance go right, they purposely go wrong;

So schismatics the plain believers quit,
And are but damned for having too much wit.
Some praise at morning what they blame at night; 430
But always think the last opinion right.
A muse by these is like a mistress used,
This hour she's idolized, the next abused;
While their weak heads, like towns unfortified,
'Twixt sense and nonsense daily change their side. 435
Ask them the cause; they're wiser still, they say;
And still to-morrow's wiser than to-day.
We think our fathers fools, so wise we grow,
Our wiser sons, no doubt, will think us so.
Once school-divines this zealous isle o'erspread; 440
Who knew most sentences, was deepest read;
Faith, gospel, all, seemed made to be disputed,
And none had sense enough to be confuted:
Scotists and Thomists, now, in peace remain, -
Amidst their kindred cobwebs in Duck-lane. 445
If faith itself has different dresses worn,
What wonder modes in wit should take their turn?
Oft, leaving what is natural and fit,
The current folly proves the ready wit;
And authors think their reputation safe, 450
Which lives as long as fools are pleased to laugh.
  Some valuing those of their own side or mind,
Still make themselves the measure of mankind:
Fondly we think we honor merit then,
When we but praise ourselves in other men. 455
Parties in wit attend on those of state,
And public faction doubles private hate.
Pride, malice, folly, against Dryden rose,
In various shapes of parsons, critics, beaus;
But sense survived, when merry jests were past; 460

c

For rising merit will buoy up at last.
Might he return, and bless once more our eyes,
New Blackmores and new Milbourns must arise:
Nay, should great Homer lift his awful head,
Zoilus again would start up from the dead.   465
Envy will merit, as its shade, pursue;
But like a shadow, proves the substance true;
For envied Wit, like Sol eclipsed, makes known
The opposing body's grossness, not its own,
When first that sun too powerful beams displays,   470
It draws up vapors which obscure its rays;
But even those clouds at last adorn its way,
Reflect new glories and augment the day.
  Be thou the first true merit to befriend;
His praise is lost, who stays, till all commend.   475
Short is the date, alas, of modern rhymes,
And 'tis but just to let them live betimes.
No longer now that golden age appears,
When patriarch-wits survived a thousand years:
Now length of fame (our second life) is lost,   480
And bare threescore is all even that can boast;
Our sons their fathers' failing language see,
And such as Chaucer is, shall Dryden be.
So when the faithful pencil has designed
Some bright idea of the master's mind,   485
Where a new world leaps out at his command,
And ready nature waits upon his hand;
When the ripe colors soften and unite,
And sweetly melt into just shade and light;
When mellowing years their full perfection give,   490
And each bold figure just begins to live,
The treacherous colors the fair art betray,
And all the bright creation fades away!

Unhappy wit, like most mistaken things,
Atones not for that envy which it brings.   495
In youth alone its empty praise we boast,
But soon the short-lived vanity is lost:
Like some fair flower the early spring supplies,
That gayly blooms, but even in blooming dies.
What is this wit, which must our cares employ?   50.)
The owner's wife, that other men enjoy;
Then most our trouble still when most admired,
And still the more we give, the more required;
Whose fame with pains we guard, but lose with ease,
Sure some to vex, but never all to please;   505
'Tis what the vicious fear, the virtuous shun,
By fools 'tis hated, and by knaves undone!
   If wit so much from ignorance undergo,
Ah, let not learning, too, commence its foe!
Of old, those met rewards who could excell,   510
And such were praised who but endeavored well:
Though triumphs were to generals only due,
Crowns were reserved to grace the soldiers, too.
Now, they who reach Parnassus' lofty crown,
Employ their pains to spurn some others down;   515
And while self-love each jealous writer rules,
Contending wits become the sport of fools:
But still the worst with most regret commend,
For each ill author is as bad a friend.
To what base ends, and by what abject ways,   520
Are mortals urged through sacred lust of praise!
Ah, ne'er so dire a thirst of glory boast,
Nor in the critic let the man be lost.
Good nature and good sense must ever join;
To err is human, to forgive, divine.   525
   But if in noble minds some dregs remain

Not yet purged off, of spleen and sour disdain;
Discharge that rage on more provoking crimes,
Nor fear a dearth in these flagitious times.
No pardon vile obscenity should find,   530
Though wit and art conspire to move your mind;
But dulness with obscenity must prove
As shameful, sure, as impotence in love.
In the fat age of pleasure, wealth, and ease,
Sprung the rank weed, and thrived with large increase: 535
When love was all an easy monarch's care;
Seldom at council, never in a war:
Jilts ruled the state, and statesmen farces writ;
Nay, wits had pensions, and young lords had wit:
The fair sat panting at a courtier's play,   540
And not a mask went unimproved away:
The modest fan was lifted up no more,
And virgins smiled at what they blushed before.
The following license of a foreign reign
Did all the dregs of bold Socinus drain;   545
Then unbelieving priests reformed the nation,
And taught more pleasant methods of salvation;
Where Heaven's free subjects might their rights dispute,
Lest God himself should seem too absolute:
Pulpits their sacred satire learned to spare,   550
And vice admired to find a flatterer there!
Encouraged thus, wit's Titans braved the skies,
And the press groaned with licensed blasphemies.
These monsters, critics! with your darts engage,
Here point your thunder, and exhaust your rage!   555
Yet shun their fault, who, scandalously nice,
Will needs mistake an author into vice;
All seems infected that the infected spy,
As all looks yellow to the jaundiced eye.

III.

Rules for the conduct of manners in a critic.   1. Candor, v. 563.
Modesty, v. 566.   Good breeding, v. 572.   Sincerity, and freedom
of advice, v. 578.   2. When one's counsel is to be restrained, v.
584.   Character of an incorrigible poet, v. 600.   And of an im-
pertinent critic, vv. 610, etc.   Character of a good critic, v. 629.
The history of criticism, and characters of the best critics.   Aristotle,
v. 645.   Horace, v. 653.   Dionysius, v. 665   Petronius, v. 667.
Quintilian, v. 670.   Longinus, v. 675.   Of the decay of criticism,
and its revival.   Erasmus, v. 693.   Vida, v. 705.   Boileau, v.
714.   Lord Roscommon, etc. v. 725.   Conclusion.

Learn then what morals critics ought to show,   560
For 'tis but half a judge's task, to know.
'Tis not enough, taste, judgment, learning, join;
In all you speak, let truth and candor shine:
That not alone what to your sense is due
All may allow; but seek your friendship, too.   565
Be silent always when you doubt your sense;
And speak, though sure, with seeming diffidence:
Some positive, persisting fops we know,
Who, if once wrong, will needs be always so;
But you, with pleasure own your errors past,   570
And make each day a critic on the last.
'Tis not enough, your counsel still be true;
Blunt truths more mischief than nice falsehoods do;
Men must be taught as if you taught them not,
And things unknown proposed as things forgot.   575
Without good breeding, truth is disapproved;
That only makes superior sense beloved.
Be niggards of advice on no pretence;
For the worst avarice is that of sense.
With mean complacence ne'er betray your trust,   580

Nor be so civil as to prove unjust.
Fear not the anger of the wise to raise;
Those best can bear reproof, who merit praise.
　'Twere well might critics still this freedom take,
But Appius reddens at each word you speak, 585
And stares, tremendous, with a threatening eye,
Like some fierce tyrant in old tapestry.
Fear most to tax an honorable fool,
Whose right it is, uncensured, to be dull;
Such, without wit, are poets when they please, 590
As without learning they can take degrees.
Leave dangerous truths to unsuccessful satires,
And flattery to fulsome dedicators,
Whom, when they praise, the world believes no more
Than when they promise to give scribbling o'er. 595
'Tis best sometimes your censure to restrain,
And charitably let the dull be vain:
Your silence there is better than your spite,
For who can rail so long as they can write?
Still humming on, their drowsy course they keep, 600
And lashed so long, like tops, are lashed asleep.
False steps but help them to renew the race,
As, after stumbling, jades will mend their pace.
What crowds of these, impenitently bold,
In sounds and jingling syllables grown old, 605
Still run on poets, in a raging vein,
Even to the dregs and squeezings of the brain,
Strain out the last dull droppings of their sense,
And rhyme with all the rage of impotence.
　Such shameless bards we have; and yet 'tis true, 610
There are as mad, abandoned critics, too.
The bookful blockhead, ignorantly read,
With loads of learned lumber in his head,

With his own tongue still edifies his ears,
And always listening to himself appears.   615
All books he reads, and all he reads assails,
From Dryden's Fables down to Durfey's Tales.
With him, most authors steal their works, or buy;
Garth did not write his own Dispensary.
Name a new play, and he's the poet's friend,   620
Nay, showed his faults — but when would poets mend?
No place so sacred from such fops is barred,
Nor is Paul's church more safe than Paul's churchyard:
Nay, fly to altars; there they'll talk you dead:
For fools rush in where angels fear to tread.   625
Distrustful sense with modest caution speaks,
It still looks home, and short excursions makes;
But rattling nonsense in full volleys breaks,
And never shocked, and never turned aside,
Bursts out, resistless, with a thundering tide.   630
    But where's the man, who counsel can bestow,
Still pleased to teach, and yet not proud to know?
Unbiassed, or by favor, or by spite;
Not dully prepossessed, nor blindly right;   634
Though learned, well-bred; and though well-bred, sincere,
Modestly bold, and humanly severe:
Who to a friend his faults can freely show,
And gladly praise the merit of a foe?
Blest with a taste exact, yet unconfined;
A knowledge both of books and human kind: 640
Generous converse; a soul exempt from pride;
And love to praise, with reason on his side?
    Such once were critics; such the happy few,
Athens and Rome in better ages knew.
The mighty Stagirite first left the shore,   645
Spread all his sails, and durst the deeps explore:

He steered securely, and discovered far,
Led by the light of the Mæonian Star.
Poets, a race long unconfined, and free,
Still fond and proud of savage liberty,   650
Received his laws; and stood convinced 'twas fit,
Who conquered nature, should preside o'er wit.
    Horace still charms with graceful negligence,
And without method talks us into sense,
Will, like a friend, familiarly convey   655
The truest notions in the easiest way.
He, who supreme in judgment, as in wit,
Might boldly censure, as he boldly writ,
Yet judged with coolness, though he sung with fire;
His precepts teach but what his works inspire.   660
Our critics take a contrary extreme,
They judge with fury, but they write with phlegm:
Nor suffers Horace more in wrong translations
By wits, than critics in as wrong quotations.
    See Dionysius Homer's thoughts refine,   665
And call new beauties forth from every line!
    Fancy and art in gay Petronius please,
The scholar's learning, with the courtier's ease.
    In grave Quintilian's copious work, we find
The justest rules, and clearest method joined: 670
Thus useful arms in magazines we place,
All ranged in order, and disposed with grace,
But less to please the eye, than arm the hand,
Still fit for use, and ready at command.
    Thee, bold Longinus! all the Nine inspire,   675
And bless their critic with a poet's fire.
An ardent judge, who zealous in his trust,
With warmth gives sentence, yet is always just;
Whose own example strengthens all his laws;

And is himself that great sublime he draws.   680
   Thus long succeeding critics justly reigned,
License repressed, and useful laws ordained.
Learning and Rome alike in empire grew;
And arts still followed where her eagles flew;
From the same foes, at last, both felt their doom,   685
And the same age saw learning fall, and Rome.
With tyranny, then superstition joined,
As that the body, this enslaved the mind;
Much was believed, but little understood,
And to be dull was construed to be good;   690
A second deluge learning thus o'er-run,
And the monks finished what the Goths begun.
   At length Erasmus, that great injured name
(The glory of the priesthood, and the shame!),
Stemmed the wild torrent of a barbarous age,   695
And drove those holy vandals off the stage.
   But see! each Muse, in Leo's golden days,
Starts from her trance, and trims her withered bays,
Rome's ancient genius, o'er its ruins spread,
Shakes off the dust, and rears his reverend head.   700
Then sculpture and her sister-arts revive;
Stones leaped to form, and rocks began to live;
With sweeter notes each rising temple rung;
A Raphael painted, and a Vida sung.
Immortal Vida: on whose honored brow   705
The poet's bays and critic's ivy grow:
Cremona now shall ever boast thy name,
As next in place to Mantua, next in fame!
   But soon by impious arms from Latium chased,
Their ancient bounds the banished Muses passed;   710
Thence arts o'er all the northern world advance,
But critic-learning flourished most in France:

The rules a nation, born to serve, obeys;
And Boileau still in right of Horace sways.
But we, brave Britons, foreign laws despised,   715
And kept unconquered, and uncivilized;
Fierce for the liberties of wit, and bold,
We still defied the Romans, as of old.
Yet some there were, among the sounder few
Of those who less presumed, and better knew,   720
Who durst assert the juster ancient cause,
And here restored wit's fundamental laws.
Such was the Muse, whose rules and practice tell,
"Nature's chief master-piece is writing well."
Such was Roscommon, not more learned than good,   725
With manners generous as his noble blood;
To him the wit of Greece and Rome was known,
And every author's merit, but his own.
Such late was Walsh — the Muse's judge and friend,
Who justly knew to blame or to commend;   730
To failings mild, but zealous for desert;
The clearest head, and the sincerest heart.
This humble praise, lamented shade! receive,
This praise at least a grateful Muse may give:
The Muse, whose early voice you taught to sing,   735
Prescribed her heights, and pruned her tender wing,
(Her guide now lost) no more attempts to rise,
But in low numbers short excursions tries:
Content, if thence the unlearned their wants may view,
The learned reflect on what before they knew: 740
Careless of censure, nor too fond of fame;
Still pleased to praise, yet not afraid to blame,
Averse alike to flatter, or offend;
Not free from faults, nor yet too vain to mend.

THOMAS GRAY.

ELEGY WRITTEN IN A COUNTRY CHURCH-YARD.

THE PROGRESS OF POESY.

ELEGY

WRITTEN IN A COUNTRY CHURCH-YARD.

———•◦•———

THE curfew tolls the knell of parting day,
  The lowing herd wind slowly o'er the lea,
The ploughman homeward plods his weary way,
  And leaves the world to darkness and to me.

Now fades the glimmering landscape on the sight,   5
  And all the air a solemn stillness holds,
Save where the beetle wheels his droning flight,
  And drowsy tinklings lull the distant folds;

Save that from yonder ivy-mantled tower
  The moping owl does to the moon complain   10
Of such as, wandering near her secret bower,
  Molest her ancient solitary reign.

Beneath those rugged elms, that yew-tree's shade,
  Where heaves the turf in many a mouldering heap,
Each in his narrow cell forever laid,   15
  The rude forefathers of the hamlet sleep.

The breezy call of incense-breathing morn,
  The swallow twittering from the straw-built shed,
The cock's shrill clarion, or the echoing horn,
  No more shall rouse them from their lowly bed.   20

For them no more the blazing hearth shall burn,
  Or busy housewife ply her evening care;
No children run to lisp their sire's return,
  Or climb his knees the envied kiss to share.

Oft did the harvest to their sickle yield, 25
  Their furrow oft the stubborn glebe has broke;
How jocund did they drive their team afield!
  How bowed the woods beneath their sturdy stroke!

Let not ambition mock their useful toil,
  Their homely joys, and destiny obscure; 30
Nor grandeur hear, with a disdainful smile,
  The short and simple annals of the poor.

The boast of heraldry, the pomp of power,
  And all that beauty, all that wealth e'er gave,
Awaits alike the inevitable hour. 35
  The paths of glory lead but to the grave.

Nor you, ye proud, impute to these the fault,
  If memory o'er their tomb no trophies raise,
Where thro' the long-drawn aisle and fretted vault
  The pealing anthem swells the note of praise. 40

Can storied urn or animated bust
  Back to its mansion call the fleeting breath?
Can honor's voice provoke the silent dust,
  Or flattery soothe the dull cold ear of death?

Perhaps in this neglected spot is laid 45
  Some heart once pregnant with celestial fire;
Hands, that the rod of empire might have swayed,
  Or waked to ecstasy the living lyre.

But knowledge to their eyes her ample page
    Rich with the spoils of time did ne'er unroll;   50
Chill penury repressed their noble rage,
    And froze the genial current of the soul.

Full many a gem of purest ray serene,
    The dark unfathomed caves of ocean bear;
Full many a flower is born to blush unseen,   55
    And waste its sweetness on the desert air.

Some village Hampden, that with dauntless breast
    The little tyrant of his fields withstood;
Some mute inglorious Milton here may rest,
    Some Cromwell guiltless of his country's blood.   60

The applause of listening senates to command,
    The threats of pain and ruin to despise,
To scatter plenty o'er a smiling land,
    And read their history in a nation's eyes,

Their lot forbade; nor circumscribed alone   65
    Their growing virtues, but their crimes confined;
Forbade to wade through slaughter to a throne,
    And shut the gates of mercy on mankind,

The struggling pangs of conscious truth to hide,
    To quench the blushes of ingenuous shame,   70
Or heap the shrine of luxury and pride
    With incense kindled at the muse's flame.

Far from the madding crowd's ignoble strife,
    Their sober wishes never learned to stray;
Along the cool sequestered vale of life   75
    They kept the noiseless tenor of their way.

Yet even these bones from insult to protect
　　Some frail memorial still erected nigh,
With uncouth rhymes and shapeless sculpture decked,
　　Implores the passing tribute of a sigh.　　　　80

Their name, their years, spelled by the unlettered muse,
　　The place of fame and elegy supply;
And many a holy text around she strews,
　　That teach the rustic moralist to die.

For who, to dumb forgetfulness a prey,　　　　85
　　This pleasing anxious being e'er resigned,
Left the warm precincts of the cheerful day,
　　Nor cast one longing lingering look behind?

On some fond breast the parting soul relies,
　　Some pious drops the closing eye requires;　　　90
Even from the tomb the voice of nature cries,
　　Even in our ashes live their wonted fires.

For thee, who mindful of the unhonored dead
　　Dost in these lines their artless tale relate:
If chance, by lonely contemplation led,　　　　95
　　Some kindred spirit shall inquire thy fate,

Haply some hoary-headed swain may say,
　　"Oft have we seen him at the peep of dawn
Brushing with hasty steps the dews away
　　To meet the sun upon the upland lawn.　　　　100

"There at the foot of yonder nodding beech,
　　That wreathes its old fantastic roots so high,
His listless length at noontide would he stretch,
　　And pore upon the brook that babbles by.

"Hard by yon wood, now smiling as in scorn,   105
    Muttering his wayward fancies he would rove,
Now drooping, woful wan, like one forlorn,
    Or crazed with care, or crossed in hopeless love.

"One morn I missed him on the customed hill,
    Along the heath and near his favorite tree;   110
Another came; nor yet beside the rill,
    Nor up the lawn, not at the wood was he;

"The next with dirges due in sad array
    Slow thro' the church-way path we saw him borne.
Approach and read (for thou can'st read) the lay,   115
    Graved on the stone beneath yon aged thorn."

THE EPITAPH.

Here rests his head upon the lap of earth
    A youth to fortune and to fame unknown.
Fair science frowned not on his humble birth,
    And melancholy marked him for her own.   120

Large was his bounty, and his soul sincere,
    Heaven did a recompense as largely send;
He gave to misery all he had, a tear,
    He gained from Heaven ('twas all he wished) a friend.

No farther seek his merits to disclose,   125
    Or draw his frailties from their dread abode,
(There they alike in trembling hope repose,)
    The bosom of his Father and his God.

D

THE PROGRESS OF POESY.

A PINDARIC ODE.

Φωνᾶντα συνετοῖσιν· ἐς
Δὲ τὸ πᾶν ἑρμηνέων χατίζει.
— PINDAR, *Olymp.* II.

I. 1.

Awake, Æolian lyre, awake,
And give to rapture all thy trembling strings.
From Helicon's harmonious springs
   A thousand rills their mazy progress take:
The laughing flowers, that round them blow,   5
Drink life and fragrance as they flow.
Now the rich stream of music winds along,
Deep, majestic, smooth, and strong,
Thro' verdant vales, and Ceres' golden reign:
Now rolling down the steep amain,   10
Headlong, impetuous, see it pour:
The rocks, and nodding groves rebellow to the roar.

I. 2.

Oh! Sovereign of the willing soul,
Parent of sweet and solemn-breathing airs,
Enchanting shell! the sullen Cares   15
   And frantic Passions hear thy soft control.
On Thracia's hills the Lord of War,

Has curbed the fury of his car,
And dropped his thirsty lance at thy command.
Perching on the sceptred hand   20
Of Jove, thy magic lulls the feathered king
With ruffled plumes, and flagging wing:
Quenched in dark clouds of slumber lie
The terror of his beak, and lightnings of his eye.

I. 3.

Thee the voice, the dance, obey,   25
Tempered to thy warbled lay.
O'er Idalia's velvet green
The rosy-crownèd Loves are seen
On Cytherea's day
With antic Sports, and blue-eyed Pleasures,   30
Frisking light in frolic measures;
Now pursuing, now retreating,
  Now in circling troops they meet:
To brisk notes in cadence beating
  Glance their many-twinkling feet.   35
Slow melting strains their Queen's approach declare:
  Where'er she turns the Graces homage pay.
With arms sublime, that float upon the air,
  In gliding state she wins her easy way:
O'er her warm cheek, and rising bosom, move   40
The bloom of young Desire, and purple light of Love.

II. 1.

Man's feeble race what ills await!
Labor, and Penury, the racks of Pain,
Disease, and Sorrow's weeping train,

And Death, sad refuge from the storms of Fate! 45
The fond complaint, my Song, disprove,
And justify the laws of Jove.
.Say, has he given in vain the heavenly muse?
Night, and all her sickly dews,
Her spectres wan, and birds of boding cry, 50
He gives to range the dreary sky:
Till down the eastern cliffs afar
Hyperion's march they spy, and glittering shafts of war.

II. 2.

In climes beyond the solar road,
Where shaggy forms o'er ice-built mountains roam, 55
The muse has broke the twilight-gloom
To cheer the shivering Native's dull abode.
And oft, beneath the odorous shade
Of Chili's boundless forests laid,
She deigns to hear the savage youth repeat, 60
In loose numbers wildly sweet,
Their feather-cinctured Chiefs, and dusky Loves.
Her track, where'er the Goddess roves,
Glory pursue, and generous Shame,
The unconquerable Mind, and Freedom's holy flame. 65

II. 3.

Woods, that wave o'er Delphi's steep,
Isles, that crown the Ægean deep,
   Fields, that cool Ilissus laves,
   Or where Mæander's amber waves
In lingering labyrinths creep, 70
   How do your tuneful echoes languish,

Mute, but to the voice of Anguish!
Where each old poetic mountain
  Inspiration breathed around:
Every shade and hallowed fountain   75
  Murmured deep a solemn sound:
Till the sad Nine in Greece's evil hour
  Left their Parnassus for the Latian plains.
Alike they scorn the pomp of tyrant Power,
  And coward Vice, that revels in her chains.   80
When Latium had her lofty spirit lost.
They sought, oh Albion! next thy sea-encircled coast.

III. 1.

Far from the sun and summer-gale,
In thy green lap was nature's darling laid,
What time, where lucid Avon strayed,   85
  To him the mighty mother did unveil
Her awful face.   The dauntless child
Stretched forth his little arms, and smiled.
This pencil take (she said) whose colors clear
Richly paint the vernal year;   90
Thine too these golden keys, immortal boy!
This can unlock the gates of joy,
Of horror that, and thrilling fears,
Or ope the sacred source of sympathetic tears.

III. 2.

Nor second he, that rode sublime   95
Upon the seraph wings of ecstacy,
The secrets of the abyss to spy.
  He passed the flaming bounds of place and time:

The living throne, the sapphire-blaze,
Where angels tremble, while they gaze,   100
He saw; but, blasted with excess of light,
Closed his eyes in endless night.
Behold, where Dryden's less presumptuous car
Wide o'er the fields of glory bear
Two coursers of ethereal race,   105
With necks in thunder clothed, and long-resounding
    pace.

III.   3.

Hark, his hands the lyre explore!
Bright-eyed Fancy hovering o'er
Scatters from her pictured urn
Thoughts, that breathe, and words, that burn.   110
But ah! 'tis heard no more —
   Oh! lyre divine, what daring spirit
   Wakes thee now? tho' he inherit
Nor the pride, nor ample pinion,
   That the Theban Eagle bear   115
Sailing with supreme dominion
   Thro' the azure deep of air:
Yet oft before his infant eyes would run
   Such forms, as glitter in the muse's ray
With orient hues, unborrowed of the sun: 120
   Yet shall he mount, and keep his distant way
Beyond the limits of a vulgar fate,
Beneath the good how far — but far above the great.

OLIVER GOLDSMITH.

THE TRAVELLER.

THE DESERTED VILLAGE.

THE TRAVELLER,

OR, A PROSPECT OF SOCIETY.

—•◦•—

REMOTE, unfriended, melancholy, slow,
Or by the lazy Scheldt or wandering Po;
Or onward, where the rude Carinthian boor
Against the houseless stranger shuts the door;
Or where Campania's plain-forsaken lies,   5
A weary waste expanding to the skies;
Where'er I roam, whatever realms to see,
My heart untravelled fondly turns to thee;
Still to my brother turns, with ceaseless pain,
And drags at each remove a lengthening chain.   10
    Eternal blessings crown my earliest friend,
And round his dwelling guardian saints attend!
Blest be that spot where cheerful guests retire
To pause from toil, and trim their evening fire:
Blest that abode where want and pain repair,   15
And every stranger finds a ready chair:
Blest be those feasts with simple plenty crowned,
Where all the ruddy family around
Laugh at the jests or pranks that never fail,
Or sigh with pity at some mournful tale;   20

Or press the bashful stranger to his food,
And learn the luxury of doing good.
   But me, not destined such delights to share,
My prime of life in wandering spent and care, —
Impelled, with steps unceasing, to pursue   25
Some fleeting good that mocks me with the view, —
That, like the circle bounding earth and skies,
Allures from far, yet, as I follow, flies;
My fortune leads to traverse realms alone,
And find no spot of all the world my own.   30
   Even now, where Alpine solitudes ascend,
I sit me down a pensive hour to spend;
And placed on high above the storm's career,
Look downward where an hundred realms appear —
Lakes, forests, cities, plains extending wide,   35
The pomp of kings, the shepherd's humbler pride.
   When thus Creation's charms around combine,
Amidst the store should thankless pride repine?
Say, should the philosophic mind disdain
That good which makes each humbler bosom vain?   40
Let school-taught pride dissemble all it can,
These little things are great to little man;
And wiser he, whose sympathetic mind
Exults in all the good of all mankind.
Ye glittering towns, with wealth and splendor crowned; 45
Ye fields, where summer spreads profusion round;
Ye lakes, whose vessels catch the busy gale;
Ye bending swains, that dress the flowery vale;
For me your tributary stores combine:
Creation's heir, the world, the world is mine!   50
   As some lone miser visiting his store,
Bends at his treasure, counts, recounts it o'er;
Hoards after hoards his rising raptures fill,

Yet still he sighs, for hoards are wanting still;
Thus to my breast alternate passions rise,　　　　55
Pleased with each good that Heaven to man supplies:
Yet oft a sigh prevails, and sorrows fall,
To see the hoard of human bliss so small;
And oft I wish amidst the scene to find
Some spot to real happiness consigned,　　　　60
Where my worn soul, each wandering hope at rest,
May gather bliss to see my fellows blest.
　　But where to find that happiest spot below
Who can direct, when all pretend to know?
The shuddering tenant of the frigid zone　　　　65
Boldly proclaims that happiest spot his own;
Extols the treasures of his stormy seas,
And his long nights of revelry and ease:
The naked negro, panting at the line,
Boasts of his golden sands and palmy wine,　　　　70
Basks in the glare, or stems the tepid wave,
And thanks his gods for all the good they gave.
　　Such is the patriot's boast where'er we roam;
His first, best country ever is at home.
And yet, perhaps, if countries we compare,　　　　75
And estimate the blessings which they share,
Though patriots flatter, still shall wisdom find
An equal portion dealt to all mankind;
As different good, by art or nature given,
To different nations makes their blessings even.　　　　80
　　Nature, a mother kind alike to all,
Still grants her bliss at labor's earnest call;
With food as well the peasant is supplied
On Idra's cliff as Arno's shelvy side;
And though the rocky-crested summits frown,　　　　85
These rocks by custom turn to beds of down.

From art more various are the blessings sent —
Wealth, commerce, honor, liberty, content.
Yet these each other's power so strong contest,
That either seems destructive of the rest.   90
Where wealth and freedom reign, contentment fails,
And honor sinks where commerce long prevails.
Hence every state, to one loved blessing prone,
Conforms and models life to that alone.
Each to the favorite happiness attends,   95
And spurns the plan that aims at other ends:
Till, carried to excess in each domain,
This favorite good begets peculiar pain.

    But let us try these truths with closer eyes,
And trace them through the prospect as it lies: 100
Here for a while my proper cares resigned,
Here let me sit in sorrow for mankind;
Like yon neglected shrub at random cast,
That shades the steep, and sighs at every blast.

    Far to the right, where Apennine ascends,   105
Bright as the summer, Italy extends:
Its uplands sloping deck the mountain's side,
Woods over woods in gay theatric pride;
While oft some temple's mouldering tops between
With venerable grandeur mark the scene.   110

    Could nature's bounty satisfy the breast,
The sons of Italy were surely blest.
Whatever fruits in different climes are found,
That proudly rise or humbly court the ground;
Whatever blooms in torrid tracts appear,   115
Whose bright succession decks the varied year;
Whatever sweets salute the northern sky
With vernal lives, that blossom but to die;
These, here disporting, own the kindred soil,

Nor ask luxuriance from the planter's toil;   120
While sea-born gales their gelid wings expand
To winnow fragrance round the smiling land.
   But small the bliss that sense alone bestows,
And sensual bliss is all the nation knows.
In florid beauty groves and fields appear;   125
Man seems the only growth that dwindles here.
Contrasted faults through all his manners reign:
Though poor, luxurious; though submissive, vain;
Though grave, yet trifling; zealous, yet untrue;
And even in penance planning sins anew.   130
All evils here contaminate the mind
That opulence departed leaves behind;
For wealth was theirs, not far removed the date,
When commerce proudly flourished through the state;
At her command the palace learned to rise,   135
Again the long-fallen column sought the skies,
The canvas glowed, beyond e'en nature warm,
The pregnant quarry teemed with human form;
Till, more unsteady than the southern gale,
Commerce on other shores displayed her sail;   140
While nought remained of all that riches gave,
But towns unmanned, and lords without a slave
And late the nation found with fruitless skill
Its former strength was but plethoric ill
   Yet still the loss of wealth is here supplied   145
By arts, the splendid wrecks of former pride;
From these the feeble heart and long-fallen mind
An easy compensation seem to find.
Here may be seen, in bloodless pomp arrayed,
The pasteboard triumph and the cavalcade,   150
Processions formed for piety and love,
A mistress or a saint in every grove.

By sports like these are all their cares beguiled;
The sports of children satisfy the child.
Each nobler aim, repressed by long control,　　　　155
Now sinks at last, or feebly mans the soul;
While low delights, succeeding fast behind,
In happier meanness occupy the mind:
As in those domes where Cæsars once bore sway,
Defaced by time and tottering in decay,　　　　160
There in the ruin, heedless of the dead,
The shelter-seeking peasant builds his shed;
And, wondering man could want the larger pile,
Exults, and owns his cottage with a smile.

My soul, turn from them, turn we to survey　　　165
Where rougher climes a nobler race display,
Where the bleak Swiss their stormy mansion tread,
And force a churlish soil for scanty bread.
No product here the barren hills afford
But man and steel, the soldier and his sword;　　170
No vernal blooms their torpid rocks array,
But winter lingering chills the lap of May;
No zephyr fondly sues the mountain's breast,
But meteors glare, and stormy glooms invest.

Yet still, even here, content can spread a charm,　175
Redress the clime, and all its rage disarm.
Though poor the peasant's hut, his feasts though small,
He sees his little lot the lot of all;
Sees no contiguous palace rear its head
To shame the meanness of his humble shed;　　　180
No costly lord the sumptuous banquet deal
To make him loathe his vegetable meal;
But calm, and bred in ignorance and toil,
Each wish contracting fits him to the soil.
Cheerful at morn he wakes from short repose,　　185

Breasts the keen air, and carols as he goes;
With patient angle trolls the finny deep;
Or drives his venturous plough-share to the steep;
Or seeks the den where snow-tracks mark the way,
And drags the struggling savage into day.   190
At night returning, every labor sped,
He sits him down the monarch of a shed;
Smiles by his cheerful fire, and round surveys
His children's looks, that brighten at the blaze;
While his loved partner, boastful of her hoard,   195
Displays her cleanly platter on the board:
And haply too some pilgrim, thither led,
With many a tale repays the nightly bed.
 Thus every good his native wilds impart,
Imprints the patriot passion on his heart;   200
And e'en those ills that round his mansion rise
Enhance the bliss his scanty fund supplies.
Dear is that shed to which his soul conforms,
And dear that hill which lifts him to the storms;
And as a child, when scaring sounds molest,   205
Clings close and closer to the mother's breast,
So the loud torrent and the whirlwind's roar
But bind him to his native mountains more.
 Such are the charms to barren states assigned;
Their wants but few, their wishes all confined.   210
Yet let them only share the praises due:
If few their wants, their pleasures are but few;
For every want that stimulates the breast
Becomes a source of pleasure when redrest.
Hence from such lands each pleasing science flies   215
That first excites desire, and then supplies;
Unknown to them, when sensual pleasures cloy,
To fill the languid pause with finer joy;

Unknown those powers that raise the soul to flame,
Catch every nerve and vibrate through the frame.   220
Their level life is but a smouldering fire,
Unquenched by want, unfanned by strong desire;
Unfit for raptures, or, if raptures cheer
On some high festival of once a year,
In wild excess the vulgar breast takes fire,   225
Till, buried in debauch, the bliss expire.
   But not their joys alone thus coarsely flow:
Their morals, like their pleasures, are but low;
For, as refinement stops, from sire to son
Unaltered, unimproved, the manners run,   230
And love's and friendship's finely pointed dart
Fall blunted from each indurated heart.
Some sterner virtues o'er the mountain's breast
May sit, like falcons cowering on the nest;
But all the gentler morals, such as play   235
Through life's more cultured walks, and charm the way,
These, far dispersed, on timorous pinions fly,
To sport and flutter in a kinder sky.
   To kinder skies, where gentler manners reign,
I turn; and France displays her bright domain.   240
Gay, sprightly land of mirth and social ease,
Pleased with thyself, whom all the world can please,
How often have I led thy sportive choir,
With tuneless pipe beside the murmuring Loire!
Where shading elms along the margin grew,   245
And freshened from the wave the zephyr flew;
And haply, though my harsh touch, faltering still,
But mocked all tune, and marred the dancer's skill;
Yet would the village praise my wondrous power,
And dance, forgetful of the noon-tide hour.   250
Alike all ages.   Dames of ancient days

Have led their children through the mirthful maze,
And the gay grandsire, skilled in gestic lore,
Has frisked beneath the burden of threescore.

So blessed a life these thoughtless realms display;   255
Thus idly busy rolls their world away.
Theirs are those arts that mind to mind endear,
For honor forms the social temper here:
Honor, that praise which real merit gains,
Or even imaginary worth obtains,   260
Here passes current: paid from hand to hand,
It shifts in splendid traffic round the land:
From courts to camps, to cottages, it strays,
And all are taught an avarice of praise.
They please, are pleased; they give to get esteem;   265
Till, seeming blessed, they grow to what they seem.

But while this softer art their bliss supplies,
It gives their follies also room to rise;
For praise too dearly loved, or warmly sought,
Enfeebles all internal strength of thought,   270
And the weak soul within itself unblest,
Leans for all pleasure on another's breast.
Hence ostentation here, with tawdry art,
Pants for the vulgar praise which fools impart;
Here vanity assumes her pert grimace,   275
And trims her robes of frieze with copper lace;
Here beggar pride defrauds her daily cheer,
To boast one splendid banquet once a year;
The mind still turns where shifting fashion draws,
Nor weighs the solid worth of self-applause.   280

To men of other minds my fancy flies,
Embosomed in the deep where Holland lies.
Methinks her patient sons before me stand,
Where the broad ocean leans against the land;

E

And, sedulous to stop the coming tide,   285
Lift the tall rampire's artificial pride.
Onward, methinks, and diligently slow,
The firm connected bulwark seems to grow;
Spreads its long arms amidst the watery roar,
Scoops out an empire, and usurps the shore —   290
While the pent ocean, rising o'er the pile,
Sees an amphibious world beneath him smile;
The slow canal, the yellow blossomed vale,
The willow-tufted bank, the gliding sail,
The crowded mart, the cultivated plain, —   295
A new creation rescued from his reign.
   Thus while around the wave-subjected soil
Impels the native to repeated toil,
Industrious habits in each bosom reign,
And industry begets a love of gain.   300
Hence all the good from opulence that springs,
With all those ills superfluous treasure brings,
Are here displayed   There much-loved wealth imparts
Convenience, plenty, elegance, and arts;
But view them closer, craft and fraud appear,   305
E'en liberty itself is bartered here.
At gold's superior charms all freedom flies;
The needy sell it, and the rich man buys;
A land of tyrants, and a den of slaves,
Here wretches seek dishonorable graves,   310
And calmly bent, to servitude conform,
Dull as their lakes that slumber in the storm.
Heavens! how unlike their Belgic sires of old —
Rough, poor, content, ungovernably bold,
War in each breast, and freedom on each brow: 315
How much unlike the sons of Britain now!
   Fired at the sound, my genius spreads her wing,

And flies where Britain courts the western spring;
Where lawns extend that scorn Arcadian pride,
And brighter streams than famed Hydaspes glide.   320
There all around the gentlest breezes stray;
There gentle music melts on every spray;
Creation's mildest charms are there combined,
Extremes are only in the master's mind!
Stern o'er each bosom reason holds her state,   325
With daring aims irregularly great;
Pride in their port, defiance in their eye,
I see the lords of human kind pass by;
Intent on high designs, a thoughtful band,
By forms unfashioned, fresh from nature's hand,   330
Fierce in their native hardiness of soul,
True to imagined right, above control,
While even the peasant boasts these rights to scan,
And learns to venerate himself as man.   334
    Thine, Freedom, thine the blessings pictured here;
Thine are those charms that dazzle and endear;
Too blessed, indeed, were such without alloy:
But fostered even by freedom ills annoy:
That independence Britons prize too high
Keeps man from man, and breaks the social tie;   340
The self-dependent lordlings stand alone,
All claims that bind and sweeten life unknown.
Here, by the bonds of nature feebly held,
Minds combat minds, repelling and repelled;
Ferments arise, imprisoned factions roar,   345
Repressed ambition struggles round her shore,
Till, overwrought, the general system feels
Its motions stop, or frenzy fire the wheels.
    Nor this the worst. As nature's ties decay,
As duty, love, and honor fail to sway,   350

Fictitious bonds, the bonds of wealth and law,
Still gather strength, and force unwilling awe.
Hence all obedience bows to these alone,
And talent sinks, and merit weeps unknown: 354
Till time may come, when, stripped of all her charms,
The land of scholars and the nurse of arms,
Where noble stems transmit the patriot flame,
Where kings have toiled and poets wrote for fame,
One sink of level avarice shall lie,
And scholars, soldiers, kings, unhonored die.   360
   Yet think not, thus when freedom's ills I state,
I mean to flatter kings, or court the great.
Ye powers of truth that bid my soul aspire,
Far from my bosom drive the low desire!
And thou, fair Freedom, taught alike to feel   365
The rabble's rage and tyrant's angry steel;
Thou transitory flower, alike undone
By proud contempt or favor's fostering sun,
Still may thy blooms the changeful clime endure!
I only would repress them to secure: 370
For just experience tells, in every soil,
That those who think must govern those that toil;
And all that freedom's highest aims can reach
Is but to lay proportioned loads on each.
Hence, should one order disproportioned grow,   375
Its double weight must ruin all below.
   O then how blind to all that truth requires,
Who think it freedom when a part aspires!
Calm is my soul, nor apt to rise in arms,
Except when fast approaching danger warms;   380
But when contending chiefs blockade the throne,
Contracting regal power to stretch their own,
When I behold a factious band agree

To call it freedom when themselves are free;
Each wanton judge new penal statutes draw,   385
Laws grind the poor, and rich men rule the law,
The wealth of climes where savage nations roam
Pillaged from slaves to purchase slaves at home;
Fear, pity, justice, indignation start,
Tear off reserve, and bare my swelling heart;   390
Till half a patriot, half a coward grown,
I fly from petty tyrants to the throne.
    Yes, brother, curse with me that baleful hour
When first ambition struck at regal power:
And thus polluting honor in its source,   395
Gave wealth to sway the mind with double force.
Have we not seen, round Britain's peopled shore,
Her useful sons exchanged for useless ore,
Seen all her triumphs but destruction haste,
Like flaring tapers brightening as they waste?   400
Seen opulence, her grandeur to maintain,
Lead stern depopulation in her train,
And over fields where scattered hamlets rose
In barren solitary pomp repose?
Have we not seen at pleasure's lordly call   405
The smiling long-frequented village fall?
Beheld the duteous son, the sire decayed,
The modest matron, and the blushing maid,
Forced from their homes, a melancholy train,
To traverse climes beyond the western main;   410
Where wild Oswego spreads her swamps around,
And Niagara stuns with thundering sound?
    Even now, perhaps, as there some pilgrim strays
Through tangled forests and through dangerous ways,
Where beasts with man divided empire claim,   415
And the brown Indian marks with murderous aim;

There, while above the giddy tempest flies,
And all around distressful yells arise,
The pensive exile, bending with his woe,
To stop too fearful, and too faint to go,   420
Casts a long look where England's glories shine,
And bids his bosom sympathize with mine.
   Vain, very vain, my weary search to find
That bliss which only centres in the mind.
Why have I strayed from pleasure and repose,   425
To seek a good each government bestows?
In every government, though terrors reign,
Though tyrant kings or tyrant laws restrain,
How small, of all that human hearts endure,
That part which laws or kings can cause or cure;   430
Still to ourselves in every place consigned,
Our own felicity we make or find :
With secret course, which no loud storms annoy,
Glides the smooth current of domestic joy.
The lifted axe, the agonizing wheel,   435
Luke's iron crown, and Damiens' bed of steel,
To men remote from power but rarely known,
Leave reason, faith, and conscience all our own.

THE DESERTED VILLAGE.

Sweet Auburn! loveliest village of the plain,
Where health and plenty cheered the laboring swain,
Where smiling spring its earliest visit paid,
And parting summer's lingering blooms delayed:
Dear lovely bowers of innocence and ease,　　　　　5
Seats of my youth, when every sport could please,
How often have I loitered o'er thy green,
Where humble happiness endeared each scene,
How often have I paused on every charm,
The sheltered cot, the cultivated farm,　　　　　10
The never-failing brook, the busy mill,
The decent church that topped the neighboring hill,
The hawthorn bush, with seats beneath the shade,
For talking age and whispering lovers made!
How often have I blessed the coming day,　　　　　15
When toil remitting lent its turn to play,
And all the village train, from labor free,
Led up their sports beneath the spreading tree
While many a pastime circled in the shade,
The young contending as the old surveyed;　　　　　20
And many a gambol frolicked o'er the ground,
And sleights of art and feats of strength went round;
And still, as each repeated pleasure tired,
Succeeding sports the mirthful band inspired;

The dancing pair that simply sought renown　　　25
By holding out to tire each other down;
The swain mistrustless of his smutted face,
While secret laughter tittered round the place;
The bashful virgin's sidelong looks of love,
The matron's glance that would those looks reprove. 30
These were thy charms, sweet village! sports like these,
With sweet succession, taught even toil to please;
These round thy bowers their cheerful influence shed:
These were thy charms — but all these charms are fled.
　　Sweet smiling village, loveliest of the lawn,　　35
Thy sports are fled, and all thy charms withdrawn;
Amidst thy bowers the tyrant's hand is seen,
And desolation saddens all thy green:
One only master grasps the whole domain,
And half a tillage stints thy smiling plain.　　　40
No more thy glassy brook reflects the day,
But, choked with sedges, works its weedy way;
Along thy glades, a solitary guest,
The hollow-sounding bittern guards its nest;
Amidst thy desert walks the lapwing flies,　　　45
And tires their echoes with unvaried cries
Sunk are thy bowers in shapeless ruin all,
And the long grass o'ertops the mouldering wall;
And trembling, shrinking from the spoiler's hand,
Far, far away thy children leave the land.　　　50
　　Ill fares the land, to hastening ills a prey,
Where wealth accumulates, and men decay.
Princes and lords may flourish, or may fade —
A breath can make them, as a breath has made:
But a bold peasantry, their country's pride,　　55
When once destroyed, can never be supplied.
　　A time there was, ere England's griefs began,

When every rood of ground maintained its man;
For him light labor spread her wholesome store,
Just gave what life required, but gave no more: 60
His best companions, innocence and health,
And his best riches, ignorance of wealth.

But times are altered; trade's unfeeling train
Usurp the land and dispossess the swain;
Along the lawn, where scattered hamlets rose,   65
Unwieldy wealth and cumbrous pomp repose,
And every want to opulence allied,
And every pang that folly pays to pride.
These gentle hours that plenty bade to bloom,
Those calm desires that asked but little room,   70
Those healthful sports that graced the peaceful scene,
Lived in each look, and brightened all the green;
These, far departing, seek a kinder shore,
And rural mirth and manners are no more.

Sweet Auburn! parent of the blissful hour,   75
Thy glades forlorn confess the tyrant's power.
Here, as I take my solitary rounds
Amidst thy tangling walks and ruined grounds,
And, many a year elapsed, return to view
Where once the cottage stood, the hawthorn grew,   80
Remembrance wakes with all her busy train,
Swells at my breast, and turns the past to pain.

In all my wanderings round this world of care;
In all my griefs — and God has given my share —
I still had hopes, my latest hours to crown,   85
Amidst these humble bowers to lay me down;
To husband out life's taper at the close,
And keep the flame from wasting by repose.
I still had hopes, for pride attends us still,
Amidst the swains to show my book-learned skill,   90

Around my fire an evening group to draw,
And tell of all I felt, and all I saw;
And as a hare whom hounds and horns pursue,
Pants to the place from whence at first she flew,
I still had hopes, my long vexations past,　　　95
Here to return — and die at home at last.
　　O blessed retirement, friend to life's decline,
Retreats from care, that never must be mine,
How happy he who crowns in shades like these
A youth of labor with an age of ease;　　　100
Who quits a world where strong temptations try,
And, since 'tis hard to combat, learns to fly!
For him no wretches, born to work and weep,
Explore the mine, or tempt the dangerous deep;
No surly porter stands in guilty state,　　　105
To spurn imploring famine from the gate;
But on he moves to meet his latter end,
Angels around befriending virtue's friend;
Bends to the grave with unperceived decay,
While resignation gently slopes the way;　　　110
And, all his prospects brightening to the last,
His heaven commences ere the world be past!
　　Sweet was the sound, when oft at evening's close,
Up yonder hill the village murmur rose.
There, as I passed with careless steps and slow,　　　115
The mingling notes came softened from below;
The swain responsive as the milk-maid sung,
The sober herd that lowed to meet their young,
The noisy geese that gabbled o'er the pool,
The playful children just let loose from school,　　　120
The watch-dog's voice that bayed the whispering wind,
And the loud laugh that spoke the vacant mind; —
These all in sweet confusion sought the shade,

And filled each pause the nightingale had made.
But now the sounds of population fail, 125
No cheerful murmurs fluctuate in the gale,
No busy steps the grass-grown footway tread,
For all the bloomy flush of life is fled.
All but yon widowed, solitary thing,
That feebly bends beside the plashy spring: 130
She, wretched matron, forced in age, for bread,
To strip the brook with mantling cresses spread,
To pick her wintry faggot from the thorn,
To seek her nightly shed, and weep till morn;
She only left of all the harmless train, 135
The sad historian of the pensive plain!
　　Near yonder copse, where once the garden smiled,
And still where many a garden flower grows wild;
There, where a few torn shrubs the place disclose,
The village preacher's modest mansion rose. 140
A man he was to all the country dear,
And passing rich with forty pounds a year;
Remote from towns he ran his godly race,
Nor e'er had changed, nor wished to change his place;
Unpractised he to fawn, or seek for power, 145
By doctrines fashioned to the varying hour;
Far other aims his heart had learned to prize,
More skilled to raise the wretched than to rise.
His house was known to all the vagrant train;
He chid their wanderings but relieved their pain; 150
The long-remembered beggar was his guest,
Whose beard descending swept his aged breast;
The ruined spendthrift, now no longer proud,
Claimed kindred there, and had his claims allowed;
The broken soldier kindly bade to stay, 155
Sat by his fire, and talked the night away,

Wept o'er his wounds, or, tales of sorrow done,
Shouldered his crutch and showed how fields were won.
Pleased with his guests, the good man learned to glow,
And quite forgot their vices in their woe;   160
Careless their merits or their faults to scan,
His pity gave ere charity began.
    Thus to relieve the wretched was his pride,
And e'en his failings leaned to virtue's side;
But in his duty prompt at every call,   165
He watched and wept, he prayed and felt for all;
And, as a bird each fond endearment tries
To tempt its new-fledged offspring to the skies,
He tried each art, reproved each dull delay,
Allured to brighter worlds, and led the way.   170
    Beside the bed where parting life was laid,
And sorrow, guilt, and pain by turns dismayed,
The reverend champion stood.   At his control
Despair and anguish fled the struggling soul;
Comfort came down the trembling wretch to raise,   175
And his last faltering accents whispered praise.
    At church, with meek and unaffected grace,
His looks adorned the venerable place;
Truth from his lips prevailed with double sway,
And fools, who came to scoff, remained to pray.   180
The service past, around the pious man,
With steady zeal, each honest rustic ran;
Even children followed with endearing wile,
And plucked his gown to share the good man's smile.
His ready smile a parent's warmth expressed,   185
Their welfare pleased him, and their cares distressed;
To them his heart, his love, his griefs were given,
But all his serious thoughts had rest in heaven.
As some tall cliff that lifts its awful form,

Swells from the vale, and midway leaves the storm,   190
Though round its breast the rolling clouds are spread,
Eternal sunshine settles on its head.
   Beside yon straggling fence that skirts the way,
With blossomed furze unprofitably gay —
There, in his noisy mansion, skilled to rule,   195
The village master taught his little school.
A man severe he was, and stern to view;
I knew him well, and every truant knew:
Well had the boding tremblers learned to trace
The day's disasters in his morning face;   200
Full well they laughed with counterfeited glee
At all his jokes, for many a joke had he;
Full well the busy whisper circling round
Conveyed the dismal tidings when he frowned.
Yet he was kind, or if severe in aught,   205
The love he bore to learning was in fault.
The village all declared how much he knew:
'Twas certain he could write, and cipher, too:
Lands he could measure, terms and tides presage,
And even the story ran that he could gauge.   210
In arguing, too, the parson owned his skill,
For, even though vanquished, he could argue still;
While words of learned length and thundering sound
Amazed the gazing rustics ranged around;
And still they gazed, and still the wonder grew,   215
That one small head could carry all he knew.
   But past is all his fame. The very spot
Where many a time he triumphed is forgot.
Near yonder thorn that lifts its head on high,
Where once the sign-post caught the passing eye,   220
Low lies that house where nut-brown draughts inspired,
Where gray-beard mirth and smiling toil retired,

Where village statesmen talked with looks profound,
And news much older than their ale went round.
Imagination fondly stoops to trace   225
The parlor splendors of that festive place:
The white-washed wall, the nicely sanded floor,
The varnished clock that clicked behind the door;
The chest contrived a double debt to pay,
A bed by night, a chest of drawers by day;   230
The pictures placed for ornament and use,
The twelve good rules, the royal game of goose;
The hearth, except when winter chilled the day,
With aspen boughs, and flowers and fennel gay;
While broken tea-cups, wisely kept for show,   235
Ranged o'er the chimney, glistened in a row.

Vain transitory splendors! could not all
Reprieve the tottering mansion from its fall?
Obscure it sinks, nor shall it more impart
An hour's importance to the poor man's heart.   240
Thither no more the peasant shall repair
To sweet oblivion of his daily care;
No more the farmer's news, the barber's tale,
No more the woodman's ballad shall prevail;
No more the smith his dusky brow shall clear,   245
Relax his ponderous strength, and lean to hear;
The host himself no longer shall be found
Careful to see the mantling bliss go round;
Nor the coy maid, half willing to be pressed,
Shall kiss the cup to pass it to the rest.   250

Yes! let the rich deride, the proud disdain,
These simple blessings of the lowly train,
To me more dear, congenial to my heart,
One native charm, than all the gloss of art:
Spontaneous joys, where nature has its play,   255

The soul adopts, and owns their first-born sway;
Lightly they frolic o'er the vacant mind,
Unenvied, unmolested, unconfined.
But the long pomp, the midnight masquerade,
With all the freaks of wanton wealth arrayed —   260
In these, ere triflers half their wish obtain,
The toiling pleasure sickens into pain;
And, even while fashion's brightest arts decoy,
The heart distrusting asks if this be joy.

    Ye friends to truth, ye statesmen who survey   265
The rich man's joys increase, the poor's decay,
'Tis yours to judge how wide the limits stand
Between a splendid and a happy land.
Proud swells the tide with loads of freighted ore,
And shouting folly hails them from her shore;   270
Hoards even beyond the miser's wish abound,
And rich men flock from all the world around.
Yet count our gains.   This wealth is but a name
That leaves our useful products still the same.
Not so the loss.   The man of wealth and pride   275
Takes up a space that many poor supplied;
Space for his lake, his park's extended bounds,
Space for his horses, equipage, and hounds:
The robe that wraps his limbs in silken sloth
Has robbed the neighboring fields of half their growth;
His seat where solitary sports are seen,   281
Indignant spurns the cottage from the green;
Around the world each needful product flies,
For all the luxuries the world supplies;
While thus the land adorned for pleasure all   285
In barren splendor feebly waits the fall.

    As some fair female unadorned and plain,
Secure to please while youth confirms her reign,

Slights every borrowed charm that dress supplies,
Nor shares with art the triumph of her eyes; 290
But when those charms are past, for charms are frail,
When time advances, and when lovers fail,
She then shines forth, solicitous to bless,
In all the glaring impotence of dress.
Thus fares the land by luxury betrayed: 295
In nature's simplest charms at first arrayed,
But verging to decline, its splendors rise,
Its vistas strike, its palaces surprise;
While, scourged by famine from the smiling land,
The mournful peasant leads his humble band, 300
And while he sinks, without one arm to save,
The country blooms — a garden and a grave.
 Where then, ah! where, shall poverty reside,
To escape the pressure of contiguous pride?
If to some common's fenceless limits strayed 305
He drives his flock to pick the scanty blade,
Those fenceless fields the sons of wealth divide,
And even the bare-worn common is denied.
 If to the city sped — what waits him there?
To see profusion that he must not share; 310
To see ten thousand baneful arts combined
To pamper luxury and thin mankind;
To see those joys the sons of pleasure know,
Extorted from his fellow-creature's woe.
Here while the courtier glitters in brocade, 315
There the pale artist plies the sickly trade;
Here while the proud their long-drawn pomps display,
There the black gibbet glooms beside the way.
The dome where pleasure holds her midnight reign,
Here, richly decked, admits the gorgeous train; 320
Tumultuous grandeur crowds the blazing square,

The rattling chariots clash, the torches glare.
Sure scenes like these no troubles e'er annoy!
Sure these denote one universal joy!
Are these thy serious thoughts?—Ah, turn thine eyes
Where the poor houseless shivering female lies.   326
She once, perhaps, in village plenty blessed,
Has wept at tales of innocence distressed;
Her modest looks the cottage might adorn,
Sweet as the primrose peeps beneath the thorn;   330
Now lost to all; her friends, her virtue fled,
Near her betrayer's door she lays her head,
And, pinched with cold, and shrinking from the shower,
With heavy heart deplores that luckless hour,
When idly first, ambitious of the town,   335
She left her wheel and robes of country brown.

   Do thine, sweet Auburn,—thine, the loveliest train,
Do thy fair tribes participate her pain?
Even now, perhaps, by cold and hunger led,
At proud men's doors they ask a little bread!   340
   Ah, no! To distant climes, a dreary scene,
Where half the convex world intrudes between,
Through torrid tracts with fainting steps they go,
Where wild Altama murmurs to their woe.
Far different there from all that charmed before   345
The various terrors of that horrid shore;
Those blazing suns that dart a downward ray,
And fiercely shed intolerable day;
Those matted woods where birds forget to sing;
But silent bats in drowsy clusters cling;   350
Those poisonous fields with rank luxuriance crowned,
Where the dark scorpion gathers death around;
Where at each step the stranger fears to wake
The rattling terrors of the vengeful snake;

F

Where crouching tigers wait their hapless prey,   355
And savage men more murderous still than they;
While oft in whirls the mad tornado flies,
Mingling the ravaged landscape with the skies.
Far different these from every former scene,
The cooling brook, the grassy-vested green,   360
The breezy covert of the warbling grove,
That only sheltered thefts of harmless love.

  Good Heaven! what sorrows gloomed that parting day,
That called them from their native walks away;
When the poor exiles, every pleasure past,   365
Hung round the bowers, and fondly looked their last,
And took a long farewell, and wished in vain
For seats like these beyond the western main,
And shuddering still to face the distant deep,
Returned and wept, and still returned to weep.   370
The good old sire the first prepared to go
To new-found worlds, and wept for others' woe;
But for himself, in conscious virtue brave,
He only wished for worlds beyond the grave.
His lovely daughter, lovelier in her tears,   375
The fond companion of his helpless years,
Silent went next, neglectful of her charms,
And left a lover's for a father's arms.
With louder plaints the mother spoke her woes,
And blessed the cot where every pleasure rose,   380
And kissed her thoughtless babes with many a tear,
And clasped them close, in sorrow doubly dear,
Whilst her fond husband strove to lend relief
In all the silent manliness of grief.

  O luxury! thou curst by Heaven's decree,   385
How ill exchanged are things like these for thee!
How do thy potions, with insidious joy,

Diffuse their pleasure only to destroy!
Kingdoms, by thee to sickly greatness grown,
Boast of a florid vigor not their own.   390
At every draught more large and large they grow,
A bloated mass of rank unwieldy woe;
Till sapped their strength, and every part unsound,
Down, down they sink, and spread a ruin round.
    Even now the devastation is begun,   395
And half the business of destruction done;
Even now, methinks, as pondering here I stand,
I see the rural virtues leave the land.
Down where yon anchoring vessel spreads the sail
That idly waiting flaps with every gale,   400
Downward they move, a melancholy band,
Pass from the shore, and darken all the strand.
Contented toil, and hospitable care,
And kind connubial tenderness, are there;
And piety, with wishes placed above,   405
And steady loyalty, and faithful love.
And thou, sweet Poetry, thou loveliest maid,
Still first to fly where sensual joys invade;
Unfit in these degenerate times of shame
To catch the heart, or strike for honest fame;   410
Dear charming nymph, neglected and decried,
My shame in crowds, my solitary pride;
Thou source of all my bliss, and all my woe,
That found'st me poor at first, and keep'st me so;
Thou guide by which the nobler arts excel,   415
Thou nurse of every virtue, fare thee well!
Farewell, and O! where'er thy voice be tried,
On Torno's cliffs, or Pambamarca's side,
Whether where equinoctial fervors glow,
Or winter wraps the polar world in snow,   420

Still let thy voice, prevailing over time,
Redress the rigors of the inclement clime;
Aid slighted truth with thy persuasive strain;
Teach erring man to spurn the rage of gain;
Teach him, that states of native strength possessed, 425
Though very poor, may still be very blessed;
That trade's proud empire hastes to swift decay,
As ocean sweeps the labored mole away;
While self-dependent power can time defy,
As rocks resist the billows and the sky.   430

ALEXANDER POPE.

1688–1744.

Apart from his career as an author, the life of Alexander Pope was uneventful. He was born May 21, 1688, in London. A few years later his father, a successful merchant, retired from business and went to Binfield, and later to Chiswick, where he died in 1717. The next year Pope, with his mother, went to live at Twickenham, twelve miles from London. The Twickenham villa stood in a park of some five acres, in the adornment of which he spent much time and money, and found one of his few diversions. Here was the famous grotto, decorated with shells and curious bits of stone, coral, and crystal, — a place well known and much admired by the wits and celebrities of the day. "Garth, Arbuthnot, Bolingbroke, Peterborough, Swift, the most brilliant company of friends that the world has ever seen," were frequent visitors. An occasional trip to London was the only separation from his mother that his filial devotion permitted; for Pope was a good son. In his veneration of his mother he becomes lovable, genuine, true.

> " Me let the tender office long engage
> To rock the cradle of reposing age,
> With lenient arts extend a mother's breath,
> Make languor smile, and soothe the bed of death,
> Explore the thought, explain the asking eye,
> And keep awhile one parent from the sky."

Such words come from the heart, and gain our affections, as his nice antitheses and rhetorical polish command our admiration and applause. Pope's mother died in 1733; "with her death the most

ennobling influence faded from the poet's life." He survived his
mother eleven years, — years crowded with literary labors and selfish plotting. His death was so peaceful that those who were
watching him did not know the moment when the end came.

Pope had no boyhood days. From his infancy he was devoted to
literature, and he spent in reading and study the time that most
boys are playing out of doors. He was sickly and deformed; so
hunch-backed that he was called "the interrogation point"; a
dwarf less than four feet high; and so weak that he could
neither dress nor undress without help. He was so sensitive to
cold that he had to be wrapped in flannels and furs, and wore
three pairs of stockings. He had to be laced in stays, and could
scarcely support himself until they were put on by his attendants.
His life was "one long disease." He had no sports, no days of
frolicsome mirth or the simple delight of boyish pranks. How
indomitable the spirit that could triumph over such defects of the
body!

The education of the poet was largely in his own hands. His
parents were Roman Catholics, and for this reason Pope was debarred from the universities and all public offices. At an early
age he was instructed by the family priest. Then he was sent to
a Romish seminary, whence he was expelled in a short time for
lampooning one of the teachers. A series of private tutors followed, but with little profit to the pupil. At twelve he decided to
direct his own education, and formed a plan of study which was
faithfully carried out, though his sole incitement was his own
desire for excellence. He read widely, dipped into authors here
and there, and studied English, French, Greek, and Latin with a
zeal that nearly ended his life. Before he was fifteen, he had
written an *Ode on Solitude,* a tragedy (acted by his playmates),
and an epic of nearly four thousand lines. He was a most pre-
cocious child, fired with ambition to win success in the world of
letters; and to the attainment of this end all his study and labor
were conformed. From his earliest days he was fond of Spenser, Waller, and Sandys. Dryden, however, was his great master.
Pope and Gray both declared that they learned versification wholly
from the works of the great poet of the Restoration period.

The choice of a profession was for Pope a limited one. His religion and his health debarred him from every public career, and condemned him to a secluded life. It was, therefore, a happy coincidence of necessity and preference that led him to adopt literature. This field attracted him. and held forth fair prospects of success. His first venture, the *Pastorals*, was published in 1709, and gained an amount of praise that this latter day finds it difficult to understand. Leslie Stephen calls them "school-boy exercises." The poet himself and the critics of his day regarded them as brilliant compositions of the highest poetic worth. The student can easily satisfy his own mind of the merits of these poems — a course that is always wisest and best.

Six years after his first publication, Pope was regarded as the greatest living poet. In this interval, the *Essay on Criticism* (1711), *Rape of the Lock* (1712, revised and republished 1714), *Windsor Forest* (1713), and the *Temple of Fame* (1715) — a paraphrase of Chaucer's *House of Fame* — were published. Comment on the *Essay* will precede the notes on that poem. The *Rape of the Lock* is a mock heroic, and the best poetical burlesque in our language. The original draft of the poem did not contain the Rosicrucian sylphs and gnomes that add so much to the grace and beauty of the present form. It was written to restore peace between the families of Lord Petre and a Miss Fermor. The young nobleman had offended by stealing a lock of the lady's hair, and her friends were not slow in expressing their indignation at his insolence. It was suggested by Caryll that a poem which would turn the affair into friendly ridicule might avert the impending unpleasantness between the two families. Pope accordingly set about the task, and the result was the most brilliant trifle in our literature. The effort was warmly praised on all sides, and "it has ever since held a kind of recognized supremacy amongst the productions of the drawing-room muse." *Windsor Forest* is less noteworthy. Nature and Pope never were good friends. His descriptions made the forests populous with pagan gods and goddesses, sanctioned by Spenser and Milton, and dragged from their Olympian abodes by the Pegasus of innumerable later versifiers. All is conventional; the warm beauty of nature could not appeal to the frigid formality of the Augustan. Of the *Temple of Fame*, Dr. Johnson declared that every part is splendid; Steele said it had a thousand beauties. It is, however, no more commendable than the other "translations" of Chaucer, and is as deservedly forgotten.

The first period of Pope's literary activity, the period to which belong the poems just enumerated, ended with the production, in 1717, of two poems of a sentimental nature — *Eloisa to Abelard* and *Elegy to the Memory of an Unfortunate Lady*. In these, Pope comes as near to true pathos as he ever did. Of genuine feeling he had but little; the most careful search will meet with scant reward. Goldsmith, Gray, or Cowper, in a single couplet, touch the heart more deeply than all the rhetorical pathos that Pope so carefully elaborated. Space makes quotation impracticable, but every student of Pope should read these poems. In them is found as "graceful an expression of poetical rhetoric as can be found in his verse."

The second period gave us his *Iliad*, — by many considered his most important contribution to our literature. The work was begun at the suggestion of Sir William Trumbull, an early friend of the poet. Swift promoted the scheme in a practical manner by securing subscriptions to the amount of a thousand guineas before the book was printed, and by introducing Pope to St. John, Atterbury, and Harley, influential Tories of that time. Addison's friend Tickell had begun a translation, but withdrew his announcement after the publication of Pope's first volume. The incident occasioned some hostility between Addison and Pope, and was the cause of the satire published some years later in the *Epistle to Dr. Arbuthnot.* Whatever Pope may have thought, — and unfortunately he cannot be believed, — he had no reason to complain. His *Homer* was praised by all, Whigs and Tories alike, and brought the translator a fortune. It is estimated that his series of the *Iliad* and *Odyssey* brought him £9000, a sum that made him independent for life. Fully as satisfactory to his vanity was the applause that greeted his venture. It made him the undisputed literary chief of the time. There were, however, some who did not concur in the popular judgment. Bentley, the greatest classical scholar of the time, said to the poet: "A very pretty poem, Mr. Pope, but you must not call it Homer." It is with this opinion that posterity agrees. Read as a narrative, Pope's *Iliad* runs so smoothly that it carries us through with no sense of weariness. Every schoolboy will read it with pleasure, and this of itself is high praise. On the other hand, it lacks the simplicity and directness of the original; it is, as one critic has expressed it, "Homer in a dress suit" Of its value to English versification, the opinion of Johnson, who said "it tuned the English tongue," may be set against that of Coleridge, who assents to this, but concludes that "the translation of Homer has been one of the main sources of that 'pseudo-poetic' diction" which he and Wordsworth struggled to put out of credit. Gray, who was a great scholar and a great poet, declared that no other version would ever equal Pope's. Three English translators preceded and many in prose and verse have followed; but among them all Pope has held his own and is most widely read.

After completing his *Homer*, Pope essayed to edit Shakespeare. For this undertaking he was poorly qualified and his failure was complete. He knew little of Elizabethan literature, he had no true sympathy with his author, and the methodical labors of an editor were not to his taste. The Shakespeare was published in six volumes in 1725. Theobald, a year later, published a criticism of Pope's work, in which he pointed out some of "the many errors committed as well as unamended by Mr. Pope." In this review, Theobald, though he praised Pope as a poet, made some strictures on him as a commentator. A much severer castigation was richly merited, but Pope, the most irritable and revengeful of authors, bitterly resented Theobald's criticism. This incident was the immediate occasion of the *Dunciad* (1728), in which Pope vented his wrath on a host of minor authors against whom his splenetic spirit had a real or fancied grievance Theobald is made the hero, — supreme dunce in the realm of dulness. The poem is full of the coarsest abuse, and illustrates Johnson's comment that Pope has a strange delight in the physically disgusting. In the midst of the vilest billingsgate, he assumes a lofty moral tone and justifies himself by the necessities of the case : in the interests of all mankind he must reprove the foolish antics of the dunces, among whom he places the scholar Bentley, the eloquent Whitfield, and the brilliant

Defoe. The poem is the very refinement of vicious cruelty. Many of those attacked would have been long since forgotten had not Pope's malignity dragged them from obscurity and wretchedness to be spitted for the fire of his revenge. The literary merit of the *Dunciad* consists in the happy strokes that here and there adorn its merciless pages. No part of it can be read with pleasure save a few lines at the end. The writers attacked — in many instances with no provocation — resented his aspersions, and the *War with the Dunces* followed. To defend himself and to provoke them still more, Pope started the *Grub Street Journal*, which existed eight years. It was characteristic of the poet that he vigorously denied all connection with this journal. He never scrupled to hazard a lie whenever it might benefit himself or injure those he considered his enemies.

The publication of the *Dunciad* marks a turning-point in Pope's career. Thenceforth his writing was of a different and more worthy style. The *Essay on Man*, a philosophical poem in four parts, was published anonymously in 1733–34, but was acknowledged in a short time. The poem is Pope's most ambitious attempt, and vows no less a purpose than that of Milton's *Paradise Lost* to vindicate the ways of God to man. The philosophy is defective; indeed, the poet seems to have no settled conviction of his own. He was in name a Roman Catholic, in reality a deist, and in practice his opinions were those that happened to be current at the time. Read as an exposition of philosophy, the poem is unsatisfactory. "Sustained reasoning is entirely beyond his power." The poetry, however, is in his best style, and amply rewards the reading. It is not a poem that is read and re-read, but there are many meteoric flashes whose brilliancy fascinates and compels more than a second perusal. The *Essay* is said to be a poetic presentation of Bolingbroke's views. This we may safely believe, for Pope acknowledges his indebtedness, and it was far from his custom to yield to another any praise that he himself might claim.

The *Moral Essays* and *Imitations from Horace* were Pope's last and best work. The personal enmities and intense bitterness that point so many of his verses are displayed, but the field is wider, and the subjects demand a more versatile treatment. Warburton says that by the original plan the *Moral Essays,* four in number,[1] were to have been included in the *Essay on Man,* to which would be added what was published as the fourth book of the *Dunciad.* Luckily, this project never passed beyond a plan. The first epistle develops Pope's theory of a ruling passion, and affords further evidence of a statement already made — that he could not sustain an argument. The second deals with a subject of which Pope had no knowledge. The theme affords him merely an opportunity to catalogue feminine foibles; the spirit of the whole is indicated in the opening couplets : —

> " Nothing so true as what you once let fall ;
> Most women have no character at all ;
> Matter too soft a lasting mark to bear,
> And best distinguished by black, brown, or fair."

The third and fourth epistles treat of false taste in the use of wealth, and covertly attack the political corruption complacently endured, if not openly promoted, by Walpole. The *Essays* abound in brilliant descriptions, caustic satire on the follies and vices of the day, and keen attacks on men of greater fame than honor. They are written in Pope's best vein, and, taken all in all, constitute a part of his work second only to the *Imitations from Horace.*

These six *Imitations* were undertaken at the suggestion of Bolingbroke, who stood sponsor for the *Essay on Man.* In them we have Pope at his best. Horace is followed only when that suits Pope's convenience. This, of course, was necessary, for, as Johnson observed, "there is an irreconcilable dissimilitude between Roman images and English manners." The poems are in a certain sense autobiographical, particularly the *Prologue* or *Epistle to Dr. Arbuth-*

---

[1] The final arrangement of the essays differs from the chronological order. The several titles and the order last adopted are given with the date of publication. (1) *Of Knowledge and Character of Men* (1733). (2) *Of the Character of Women* (1735) ; (3) *Of the Use of Riches* (1732) (4) *Of the Use of Riches* (1731). These were published as epistles, and others not belonging to the series were later added, though written much earlier.

not, in which may be found the famous satire on Addison and the exquisite lines referring to the poet's mother. The force of many of the portraits is lost now in the general ignorance of the persons satirized; but "the point and venom are there, and will not be lost so long as fuller knowledge is accessible."

Some mention must be made of Pope's correspondence, an artificial, rhetorical lot of letters, by no means worth the lying and deceit which attended their publication. "The elaborate scheme he planned and carried out, so as to appear in the light of being forced for his own protection to publish this correspondence, reads like the plot of a cheap and particularly villanous melodrama." The whole miserable story may be found in Dilke's *Papers of a Critic*, or in Volume I. of Elwin's edition of *Pope*. In the history of literature, there is no incident that, for mendacity, treachery, and meanness, can parallel the revolting duplicity of Pope's conduct. The deformities of his body seem to have warped his soul. Of his conduct throughout life the same thing must be said. Petty intrigues were his delight; deceit was preferred when the truth would have served him better. No man, he tells us, can be known save by discovery of his ruling passion. And for him an inordinate vanity and an insatiate love of praise made it, —

"Enough if all around him but admire."

Pope's contemporaries ranked him among the peers of song. In later days some critics have denied him the name of poet, while others have sanctioned the judgment of the Augustans. Byron, Scott, and Ruskin give him the warmest praise; and all agree that on his own ground he stands alone. The point to determine is simply what Pope's peculiar province is. His defects are of such nature that, no matter how great his merits may be, his entrance into the first rank — that of Chaucer, Shakespeare, and Spenser — is forbidden. His genius was not creative; his imagination has rhetorical power, but no passion; he cannot sing; his best thoughts but engage the mind, and never reach the heart He has no intense feeling, no height nor depth; he cannot see the glory of nature nor hear her melodies, — "a primrose was no more to him than it was to Peter Bell." There are, however, great merits in his verse, and these entitle him to a high place in the second order of poets. A lively fancy, rhetorical skill, an almost unparalleled power in satire, and a consummate mastery of words are not gifts to be lightly esteemed. His genius was hampered by the servile spirit of his time, and he was not a man who could rise superior to its influence.

ESSAY ON CRITICISM.

The aim of the *Essay* is to present the accepted principles of poetic and critical composition. Its value does not consist at all in the originality of the precepts, but wholly in the skill with which they are presented. Pope's work had been preceded by the *Ars Poetica* of Horace, the *Poetica* of Vida, *L'Art Poétique* of Boileau. In English, also, there had been an *Essay on Satire* and *Essay on Poetry*, by the Earl of Mulgrave; an *Essay on Translated Verse*, by Roscommon (who also translated Horace's *Ars Poetica*); and an *Essay upon Unnatural Flights in Poetry*, by Lord Lansdowne. Pope's *Essay* embodies all that had gone before. It gives us the result of an intelligent study of Greek and Latin critical writing, and summarizes the works of the French and English critics of the seventeenth century "It may be described as a literary patchwork;" or, better, as a compendium of criticism.

The *Essay* was published in 1711, when Pope was in his twenty-fourth year. He assigns the poem to 1707, but it must be remembered that Pope's excessive vanity led him always to pretend to a precocity greater than he possessed. This foible inclines us to accept the year 1709 as the date of composition; and in defence it may be urged that in every edition, up to 1743, this date (1709) is given. Pope's "ruling passion" has occasioned his many editors no small difficulty in assigning dates to his compositions.

Whatever the date, the *Essay* is a marvel, when the youth of the writer is considered. Horace, Vida, and Boileau were old men when they advanced their precepts of criticism. The word *Essay* in the title accords well with the author's years and suggests that the poem is merely a contribution to the subject and not a methodi-

cal treatise. There is, however, sufficient method to give coher-
ence to the many details. Three parts are clearly indicated: the
first (ll. 1–201) treats of the art of criticism; the second (ll. 202–
560) analyzes the ten causes of wrong judgment in criticism; the
third (ll. 560 *ad fin.*) discusses the qualities that should distinguish
the true critic. There is no difficulty in finding fault with the
composition. It has many repetitions, some inconsistencies, and
a few irrelevant lines. The metre is sometimes faulty, there is a
monotony of rhyme, and an unpleasant recurrence of a few overworked words. A more serious fault is the exaltation of Walsh,
Sheffield, and Roscommon above Chaucer, Spenser, Shakespeare,
and Milton. Nowhere, however, can be found a better guide for
the critic. The *Essay* abounds in terse felicitous expressions furnished by Pope in their final form. Scarcely a page but contains
aphorisms marked by a shrewdness and nicety that have made
them the literary stock of many to whom the *Essay* is unknown.
St. Beuve, the greatest of French critics, pronounced it quite as
good as the work of Horace or Boileau. Certain it is that no composition has ever exercised so potent an influence upon contemporary writers; nor could there be a surer evidence of its worth than
the acceptance of its style and precepts by all subsequent writers
until the revolt against formality successfully conducted by Wordsworth and Coleridge.

4. Sense: supply the word 'critical' and the meaning will be
clear.

5. in that . . . in this : Pope early drags in his favorite antithesis.
The mannerism is one he was not slow to detect and condemn in
others. Cf. *Epistle to Dr. Arbuthnot*, ll. 323–325.

6. Censure . is used with a meaning now obsolete. Cf 1 16,
where the word occurs with the force it has to-day

9 ff. The simile of the watches is probably borrowed from the epilogue of Suckling's *Aglaura*. The drama is not easily accessible and
the lines are therefore quoted : —

> " But as when an authentic watch is shown,
> Each man winds up and rectifies his own,
> So in our very judgments "

11 ff. Pope here follows Longinus, who places the great critic almost on a level with a great original genius. There have been fewer great poets than great critics, and modern judgment discriminates between talent, the critic's power, and genius, the poet's endowment.

15. Such ... who: modern idiom requires 'as' for the correlative of 'such.' In Pope's time 'who,' 'which,' or 'that,' might be used. Cf. ll. 385 and 511.   In **themselves** is an ambiguity. Pope has a note on this passage, quoting from Pliny: "De pictore, sculptore, fictore, nisi artifex, judicare non potest," "Concerning a painter, a sculptor, a maker of statues, no one except an artist is competent to judge." Johnson did not think this good reasoning. "You *may* abuse a tragedy, though you cannot write one. You *may* scold a carpenter who has made you a bad table, though you cannot make a table. It is not your trade to make tables."

17. Wit: this word was in common use among the writers of Pope's day. It occurs at least forty-nine times in this *Essay* and has no less than seven distinct though closely related meanings. *Wit* is derived from the Anglo-Saxon *witan*, 'to know.' The primary meaning is (1) the 'intellect,' and (2) 'knowledge.' The first was later narrowed to (3) 'judgment' and (4) 'fancy' or what to-day we name 'imagination.' From 'imagination' came (5) products of imagination, *i.e.* certain analogies that the mind perceives in nature, and (6) far-fetched resemblances between things apparently dissimilar. Lastly, it denotes (7) those who detect such analogies. In the present line 'wit' means knowledge. Hereafter, when the word is used, the student may refer to this note and ascertain the meaning required by the context.

20. Pope quotes from Cicero, *De Oratore*, Bk. III. Chap. 50   The passage translated reads: "All men, by a certain tacit sense, without any artistic skill or power of reason, can determine what is right and wrong in the arts and in reasoning."

23-25. Triplets occur eight times in this *Essay*. After the *Iliad*, Pope ceased to use them to any extent. None are found in the *Essay on Man*. The triplet, like the Alexandrine, is properly used to mark a climax, or, rarely, to break the monotony of the couplet. It was introduced by the Elizabethan poets and first used to excess by Dryden.

26. Maze of schools: confusion of doctrines

30. Modern idiom of course does not permit this construction

Pope often compels his pronouns to bear unaccustomed burdens. Cf. ll. 15, 35, and 169. One unhappy result of the polishing to which he submitted all his compositions may be noticed here. In the first edition, this couplet read : —

> "Those hate as rivals all that write : and others
> But envy wits as eunuchs envy lovers."

The corrected copy gives us the rhymes 'write' and 'spite' twice in six lines. In the prologue to Part II. of Dryden's *Conquest of Granada* is the following couplet . —

> "They who write ill, and they who ne'er durst write
> Turn critics out of mere revenge and spite."

34. Mævius . is usually coupled with Bavius. They were wretched poets, who lived at the time of Virgil and Horace. They would never have been known had not Virgil immortalized them in the third *Eclogue*. Their names, too, furnished titles for two poems, the *Baviad* and the *Mæviad*, in which William Gifford (1756–1826), editor of the *Quarterly Review*, attacked the sentimental poetasters who constituted the Della-Cruscan school. The verses of these poets, though characterized by fulsome affectation and the vilest taste, were exceedingly popular for a time.

38. The order of words in this verse illustrates the grammatical inaccuracies so numerous in this poem.

39. The mule is a hybrid between the horse and ass, and is barren.

40-43 The construction here is not elliptical nor is it ungrammatical. Take "those half-learned witlings" as object and turn the whole into prose order. The passage becomes clear, though inelegant.

44 Tell means to count. So in Milton's *L'Allegro*, ll. 67–68. See also *Exodus*, v 8. Cf. modern phrase 'all told.' The form 'em has no relation with our contraction from 'them,' but is a corruption of *hem*, an old dative plural of *he*.

45. The faulty construction obscures the meaning. Pope meant to say that to talk as much as one vain wit does, would tire a hundred ordinary tongues.

48–49 These lines are adapted from Horace, *Ars Poetica*, ll 38 ff "You who write should take a subject adapted to your powers ; and you should consider at length what your shoulders can carry and what they cannot "

50. Warburton explains the " point where sense and dulness meet " as that at which the critic's taste and judgment part company. The following paragraph, he says, ll. 51–67, gives the reason for this conclusion, *i.e.* that "the mental faculties are so constituted that one of them can never excel but at the expense of the others." In general this is probably true, but the psychology is more popular than scientific. Macaulay, Johnson, Dante, and Milton might be cited as exceptions.

53. Pretending : ambitious or aspiring.   Note the repetition of the rhymes in ll. 60 and 61.

61. The maxim of Hippocrates, " Life is short but art is long," has been adapted by most of our poets.

62. Peculiar   means particular.

64. Can you illustrate this statement ?

68 ff. Each student must settle for himself a question that has vexed several generations of editors.   Leslie Stephen, *Life of Pope,* says Pope would have been puzzled to tell precisely what he meant by his antithesis between nature and art.   Mr. Courthope defends the poet with great ability.   The advice to critics may be simplified as follows : Since nature prescribes the limits for true poetry, the critic should frame his judgment by her unvarying laws.   These laws are nature methodized, their true exemplification is found in the old poets, Homer and Virgil, and their purest statement in the old critic, Aristotle, whose nearness to nature enabled them to copy her more closely, and we are nearest nature when we copy them most closely (ll. 68–140).

73   This line, by its loose generality, contradicts the accepted notion that the **end** of art is to produce pleasure by means of the imagination.   The logical **test**, therefore, would be the degree of success attained.

75. Line seventy-nine makes clear the possible ambiguity of this line.

80–81   Wit : has two meanings in these lines.   The next couplet expands and illustrates the meaning of this distich.

86. The winged courser · *i.e.* Pegasus.   **Generous** : has here its root (*gener*) force of thoroughbred, hence mettlesome.   Cf. George Eliot, *How Lisa loved the King*, stanza II.

G

88. The canons of criticism were not devised by critics, but were deduced from the works of the great masters, whose inspiration was nature and whose work may therefore be identified with nature. The student would do well to read Johnson's remarks on this subject in the *Rambler,* No. 158, Sept. 21, 1758.

90. But: means only, and is incorrectly placed. That nature is restrained only by such laws as she herself ordained is not intelligible. Longinus tells us, in the *Treatise on the Sublime,* that the restraints of art are what curb nature.

96. The immortal prize: at the Greater or City Dionysia, the chief spring festival of the Athenians, there were dramatic contests at which prizes were awarded to the writers of successful comedies and tragedies.

98 The construction answers to the Latin ablative absolute. The student should notice the unidiomatic English in the expression " given from examples."

105. The subject of **wooed** and antecedent of **who** must be supplied. Cf. note to l. 30.

106. The thought of these lines seems to have been suggested by Dryden's dedication of his *Translation of Ovid* See also Johnson's opinion in the *Rambler,* No. 3, March 27, 1750.

107. Cf. l. 347.

108. A licensed apothecary in England is allowed to practise medicine as well as to sell drugs. The abbreviation is sanctioned by old dramatists. One of Heyward's *Four P's* is a ' poticary.'

109. Doctor's bills: prescriptions.

112. This half sneer at the editors of ancient texts finds unrestrained expression in the *Dunciad,* Bk. IV. l. 199 ff.

117. Cf. *Dunciad,* Bk. IV. ll. 251, 252.

120. Fable: *i.e* the plot.

124–125. These lines are adapted from Horace, *Ars Poetica,* ll. 268, 269. " Study Greek examples by night and day." Byron, *Hints from Horace,* has : —

> " Ye who seek finished models, never cease
> By day and night to read the works of Greece."

129. Mantuan Muse . Virgil. Publius Virgilius Maro is the poet's full name. He was born near Mantua, in Cisalpine Gaul, B.C. 70.

130. Pope, in a note, gives the anecdote on which he based these lines: "It is a tradition preserved by Servius, that Virgil began with writing a poem of the Alban and Roman affairs, which he found above his years, and descended first to imitate Theocritus on rural subjects, and afterward to copy Homer in heroic poetry."

138. Stagirite. Aristotle, who was born B C. 384, at Stagira, a seaport town of Chalcidice. Among his extant works are the *Poetics* and *Rhetoric.* The word 'Stagirite' (accented as here) occurs in the other lines in the *Essay.* It should, however, be Stăgīrite. Cf. l. 271, where Pope condemns Dennis for the very thing which here is reckoned in Virgil's praise.

143 "A Painter may make a better face than ever was; But he must doe it by a kinde of Felicity (As a Musician that maketh an excellent Ayre in Musicke) And not by Rule." (Bacon's essay *Of Beauty.*) With this passage, cf. Boileau, *Art of Poetry,* l. 78 ff

152. Brave disorder: the phrase occurs in the translation of Boileau's *Art of Poetry* by Soame, Canto II., discussion of the ode, ll. 14-15. Sir William Soame made a translation of *L'Art Poétique,* and at Dryden's suggestion the allusions were adapted to English authors.

159. In Dryden's *Arungzebe,* Act IV., occurs a line which may have suggested this one: —

"Mean soul, and dar'st not gloriously offend."

162. Pope is again indebted to Dryden. The expression may be found in the *Discourse on Epic Poetry,* which formed the preface of his translation of the *Æneid.* Apollo, answering a charge of anachronism against "his son Virgil," says that "being a monarch, he had a dispensing power and pardoned him." The right to exempt individuals from the penal laws was freely exercised by Henry VII. and continued unchallenged until the time of Charles II. The attempt of James II. to enforce this prerogative precipitated the revolution (1688) by which the Stuarts lost the throne of England. The Bill of Rights (1699) declared the dispensing power to be illegal. A full and exceedingly interesting account may be found in Macaulay's *History of England.*

169. Cf. note on l. 30.

170. Faults: the rhyme is not false, for the *l* was not sounded at Pope's time. The same rhymes occur at least twice in Soame's translation of Horace, Cantos III. and IV.

172-174. These lines are taken directly from Horace, l. 360 ff Cf. Byron, *Hints from Horace*, ll. 571-576 ; also Soame and Dryden's Trans. of *L'Art Poétique*, Canto I. ll. 171-178.

180. Homer nods : Horace, l. 359, has : —

> " Vexed on the other hand, if now and then
> Short fits of slumber creep on Homer's pen."
>
> —Trans. by Howes.

Roscommon is less respectful : —

> " Whose railing heroes, and whose wounded gods,
> Make some suspect he snores as well as nods."
>
> — *Essay on Translated Verse*, ll. 138-140.

Cf. Byron, *Hints from Horace*, ll. 569-570.

182 Mr. Collins notes that this line is transposed literally from Roscommon's epilogue to *Alexander the Great.*

183-184. Bishop Warburton says that reference is here made to "the four great causes of ravage amongst ancient writings." These were : (*a*) the destruction of the Alexandrine and Palatine libraries by fire ; (*b*) the fiercer rage of critics like Zoilus, Mævius, and their followers against wit ; (*c*) the irruption of the barbarians into the empire in the fifth century ; (*d*) the long reign of monkish ignorance and superstition

189. Cf. Dryden, *Religio Laici*, l. 80 , also Virgil, *Æneid*, Bk. VI. l. 649

194 The word **must** is equivalent to ' can.' No student can appreciate the force of this word without looking up its history. See Skeat's *Etymological Dictionary*, Sweet's *Short Historical English Grammar*, sec. 721, and Abbott's *Shakespearian Grammar*, sec. 314 ; also *Century Dictionary*

204. Cf. *Essay on Man*, Epistle II. ll. 282-294.

206. Recruits : *i e.* supplies.

207-208. The physiology in this passage is of course the sheerest nonsense. The order is faulty   Certainly souls do not stand in need of blood and spirits

213-214 With these lines, cf. Boileau, *L'Art Poétique*, ll. 49-58 In Soame and Dryden's Trans., ll. 47-56.

215. A little learning : cf. Bacon's essay *Of Atheism,* for the probable source of this passage.

216. Pierian spring · Pierides was a name for the nine muses. The name was derived probably from Pieria, a place in Thessaly where the muses were worshipped There is a legend that the daughter of Pierus challenged the muses to a contest in singing. When the muses began, Mt. Helicon gradually rose until it was stopped by a kick from Pegasus, and from the place he kicked, the spring Hippocrene bubbled forth.

225 ff. "This famous simile," Johnson said, "is perhaps the best that English poetry can show." His comments should be read by every student. See *Lives of the Poets*, "Pope." An eminent critic of our own day calls it a "poor simile" and says it is pretty well forgotten. See Leslie Stephen's *Life of Pope*, p 27 In either case the figure was not original with Pope He found the germ of it in *An Hymn of the Forest Fair* (*Flowers of Zion*) by Drummond of Hawthornden. This was first pointed out by Warton.

234 The solecism is occasioned by the ellipsis. 'Such' and 'same,' used as correlatives, are avoided in poetic diction Pope's remedy would have been, not to expand the sentence, but to recast it

239. In such lays: there is here a Latin force of the preposition in, 'in the case of.' Or there may be the double construction, called by rhetoricians anacoluthon. "Such lays we cannot blame," or "In such lays we cannot blame anything" Pope has a combination of the two ideas. It was his mania for polishing and revising that exposed the poet to confusions such as this. Cf., with this passage, Boileau's *L'Art Poétique*, Canto I. ll. 72–73, Soame and Dryden's Trans., ll. 71–72

243 ff. Cf. Horace, *Ars Poetica*, ll. 32–35, Howes' Trans., ll. 50–57.

247. Dome: either the Pantheon or St. Peter's at Rome.

251. Appear: should the form be plural?

258-262. Cf. Horace, *Ars Poetica*, ll. 347–353, and Byron, *Hints from Horace*, ll. 557–570.

261. Verbal: is here equivalent to verbose, a sense of the word now obsolete.

263-266. Johnson (*Rambler*, No. 158) says, "Criticism has not yet attained the certainty and stability of science." Students will recall the attitude of Matthew Arnold toward criticism. In Pope's time and long after, critical writing was devoted largely to an expression of individual preferences.

267. La Mancha's knight · Don Quixote. The incident here described is not taken from Cervantes, but from a continuation of his romance by an author who assumed the name of Avellaneda and possibly may have been Lope de Vega. This second part was translated and remodelled by Le Sage (1668-1747), author of *Gil Blas.* It may interest the student to know that Cervantes and Shakespeare died on the same day (April 23, 1616).

270. John **Dennis** (1657-1734) : is one of several writers known to posterity mainly by reason of Pope's attacks on them. Dennis was possessed of a narrow, pedantic scholarship and an abusive critical power. He wrote several plays (see l. 585), but his best work is in his *Original Letters, Familiar, Moral, and Critical* It was his attack on Addison's *Cato* that indirectly caused the breach between Pope and Addison. (See Macaulay's *Essay on Addison,* ed. by S Thurber, pp. 292-294.) The quarrel between Dennis and Pope began when Dennis criticised the *Rape of the Lock,* and continued with great bitterness until after his death. He was blind and poverty-stricken late in life, and in 1733 Vanbrugh's *Provoked Husband,* with a prologue by Pope, was acted for his benefit.

276. Unities: the dramatic unities were deduced from Aristotle's *Poetics* and Greek dramas. They were three in number, — time, place, and action. The first required that the events of a drama should be such as would occur in a single day ; the second forbade shifting the scene from place to place ; the third eliminated everything that did not bear directly on the catastrophe. The unities were formulated by Corneille in three essays, published in 1659.

287. Form short ideas: their ideas fall short of the truth, and as critics of art they become offensive as persons of eccentric behavior in general society.

289-292. The school of poets whose characteristics are given in these lines was called metaphysical or fantastic, and included Donne, Crashaw, Cowley, Waller, and Cleveland. They lived in Milton's time. Dr. Johnson, in his *Life of Cowley,* gave a clear analysis of their style.

297-298. The thought of this couplet is not quite clear. The argument seems to be that the wit of the fantastic school was false, because we do not see in nature the quaint analogies fancied by Crashaw or Cowley. The image reflected by the poet should be one that the common man could see as well ; the poet's advantage consists in his superior power of expressing what he sees. Read Lowell's *Essay on Pope.* For the thought here, Pope was indebted to both

Dryden and Boileau. Lines 311–319 form a good commentary on this couplet. Cf. Buckingham, *Essay on Poetry*, 270, 271 : —

> " Humor is all ; wit should be only brought
> To turn agreeably some proper thought. "

Also *Spectator*, No. 253, a review of the *Essay*. Addison quotes from Boileau the part referred to above.

299. Supply the ellipsis carefully.

305. The allusion in this paragraph is probably to the euphuists, the gallants of England in the days of Elizabeth. The interested student may find what this style was by reading a few sentences from John Lilly's *Euphues and his England*, or from Lodge's *Rosalynde*.

306. Pope takes no pains to hide his contempt for women. See *Moral Essays*, Epistle II.

318. Still: cf. l. 32. The meaning is Elizabethan. The word fills out the line, and has no other use.

319. Decent: cf. Goldsmith, *The Deserted Village*, l. 12 and note.

322. Sort: means agree with. The verb is, of course, usually transitive.

324. This charge has been brought against Livy and Sallust ; and might be urged against Spenser, for the diction of his *Shepherd's Calendar*. In the preface to these eclogues he tells us that he purposely employed archaic forms, and gives good reason for his choice. **Pretence :** is here used in a good sense, denoting a claim to merit or dignity. Cf. Cowper, *Truth*, l 93.

328. Fungoso : a character in Ben Jonson's *Every Man out of his Humor* (1599). The *dramatis personæ* describes him as " a student, one that has revelled in his time, and follows the fashion afar off, as a spy." He is called "unlucky," because of his experiences in attempting to imitate in dress and manner Fastidious Brisk, a character aptly described by his name.

329. Sparks : " A spark is a lively, showy, splendid, gay man. The term is commonly applied in contempt " Johnson's *Dictionary*.

332. Doublet: this was an outer garment worn by men. Sometimes it had skirts, but more often did not. In the time of Charles I. it became an under garment, lost its sleeves, and at last developed into the modern waistcoat.

337. Numbers : in the sense of verse is imitated from Latin. Cf. *Epistle to Dr. Arbuthnot*, l. 128.

345 The student will not fail to notice how well in this and the following lines Pope illustrates the fault he condemns. To avoid the unpleasant effect from juxtaposition of open vowels, poets often made use of elisions (cf. ll. 200, 327). In our day, the final vowel of the first word is slurred rather than altogether elided. For this reason, the many elisions that occurred in Pope's text have not been preserved.

346. The exact meaning of **expletives** is clear when one considers why oaths are so called.

347. In 1667, Dryden, in his *Essay on Dramatic Poesy*, wrote of some obscure author: "He is a very leveller in poetry; he creeps along with ten little words in every line . . . and helps out his numbers with all the pretty expletives he can find."

350. Pope took his examples of trite rhymes from Hopkin's *Translation of Ovid's Metamorphoses*, Bk. XI :—

> "No tame nor savage beast dwells there ; no breeze
> Shakes the still boughs, or whispers through the trees:
> Here easy streams with pleasing murmurs creep,
> At once inviting and assisting sleep."

But see *Eloisa to Abelard*, ll. 159, 160 , *Winter*, ll. 61, 62, 79, 80 ; *Essay on Man*, I ll. 271, 272.

356. Alexandrine is illustrated in the next line. The name is taken from the *Roman d'Alexandre*, a poem of the twelfth century, written in this metre. The poem was begun by Lambert le Court and finished by Alexandre de Bernay, whence some derive the name of the verse. It was used freely by Cowley and Dryden, and is found frequently in Pope's early poems.

361. Sir John **Denham** (1615-1668) and Edmund **Waller** (1605-1687). were poets of mediocre talents, greatly overestimated by their contemporaries and immediate followers. Denham's fame rests on *Cooper's Hill;* Waller is best known by his lyrics. The one beginning *Go, Lovely Rose*, the lines *On a Girdle*, and the verses on old age are not likely to be forgotten. These poets may be regarded as the forerunners of the school that found its apotheosis in Pope.

365. Cf. Roscommon's *Essay on Translated Verse*, l 342. The thought and imagery of the following passage are taken from Vida's *Art of Poetry*, Bk. III. Every student should read Johnson's comment on this passage, *Life of Pope.* Valuable also are his remarks in the *Rambler*, No. 92, Feb. 2, 1751

370. Ajax: twice hurls "crags." See *Iliad*, VII. 268 ff.; Bryant's Trans., 316 ff.; and XII. l. 380 ff.; Bryant's Trans., l. 451 ff

372. Camilla· the virgin queen of the Volscians; assisted Turnus in his war against Æneas See *Æneid*, VII. l. 808 ff. Pope's lines are variations of Dryden's translation. See Bk. VII. l. 1094 ff.

374 Timotheus The allusion is to Dryden's *Alexander's Feast.* Pope in this passage presents a good, spirited summary of his master's greatest lyric.

376. The son of Libyan Jove: this refers to the legend that Alexander the Great was a son of Zeus Ammon, a Libyan god.

383. John Dryden (1631–1700) was Pope's poetical father. "I learned versification wholly from Dryden's works, who had improved it much beyond any of our former poets." (Spence's *Anecdotes*, p. 46.) Pope, though but twelve years old when Dryden died, saw him once. See Johnson's *Life of Pope.*

384 Such . . who: cf. note to l. 15

391. Admire: exactly the Latin *admirari*, to feel astonished. Cf. Horace, *Epistle* I. VI. 1–2.   **Approve**: is used in the sense of test. Cf. *King Henry IV.*, Part I Act IV. sc 1. l. 9.

394. Foreign writers· Pope originally wrote "*French* writers." The reference is to the dispute about the relative importance of ancient and modern writers, which originated in France late in the seventeenth century and soon spread to England. It occasioned the famous Phalaris controversy and Swift's satire, *Battle of the Books.* See Macaulay's *Essay on Sir William Temple*, and De Quincey's *Essay on Bentley*

397. To one small sect· this line gave offence to the Roman Catholics, against whom the sarcasm is directed When the same sect objected to the next line, Pope said that the 'they' referred to 'some,' l. 394. See Stephen's *Life of Pope*, p. 174.

403 Enlights: see *Century Dictionary.*

423. Cf. note to l. 170.

428: Schismatics: was accented on the antepenult in Pope's time. What peculiarity does its present accent show?

435. 'Twixt sense and nonsense: describes this couplet no less than it does the **weak heads.**   **Towns unfortified** frequently change sides, but they do not hover between sense and nonsense.

441. The reference here is to the *Book of Sentences* (1159), a compilation of religious doctrines gathered from the early church fathers. It was arranged by Peter Lombard, Bishop of Paris, who was known as the Master of Sentences. The book became the manual of the schools.

444. Scotists and Thomists : the student can learn what a Scotist was by looking up the etymology of the word "dunce." "Thomists" were followers of Thomas Aquinas (1227–1274), "the Angelic Doctor." He was of the Dominican order, and was a famous lecturer in Paris and in Italian universities. He wrote a learned commentary on Peter Lombard's *Book of Sentences.* An account of the war between the Scotists and Thomists may be found in Milman's *History of Latin Christianity*, Vol. IX. Chap. III., and in Hallam's *Introduction to the Literature of Europe*, Chap. I.

445. Pope, in a note, explains that "Duck Lane was a place where old and second hand books were sold formerly, near Smithfield."

448 ff Here is a crux. Warburton says, "The writer, when he finds his readers disposed to take ready wit on the standard of current folly, never troubles himself to think of better payment." Thomas Arnold explains thus, "He who paints current follies gains laughter and applause; but after a few years the joke seems frigid, and the wit forced."

459. Of the parsons who rose against Dryden, Jeremy Collier and Luke Milbourne may be mentioned ; the critics were Thomas Shadwell and Elkanah Settle ; the beaux were Guy Villiers, Duke of Buckingham, and John Wilmot, Earl of Rochester. Dryden's relations with these men can be understood best by reference to Saintsbury's *Life of Dryden* and Johnson's *Life of Dryden.*

463. Sir Richard Blackmore wrote *The Creation*, a didactic poem in seven books, highly praised by Addison and Johnson , an epic poem on *King Alfred;* and a sacred poem, *The Redeemer.* He was physician to William III. and to Queen Anne. His biography may be found in Johnson's *Lives of the Poets*

465. Zoilus · is called the "scourge of Homer," because of the severity with which he attacked the author of the *Iliad* and *Odyssey.* Plato also incurred his censure. He was probably a contemporary of Demosthenes (B c. 382–322).

480. Cf Milton, *Lycidas*, l. 70 ff.

483. Both Dryden and Pope modernized part of Chaucer's *Tales.*

The fact is, however, that Chaucer is to-day more popular than either of his translators. Many authors have sought to secure their work for posterity by the use of Latin Bacon for this reason translated his work into Latin. Warton quotes from Waller's *Of English Verse :* —

> " Poets that lasting marble seek
> Must carve in Latin or in Greek ;
> We write in sand : our language grows,
> And like the tide our work o'erflows."

484 ff. Pope amused himself with painting, as Milton did with music. Cf. *Epistle to Jervas.* See also the concluding lines of Dryden's *Epistle to Sir Godfrey Kneller.*

506–507. This couplet is not at all clear That the vicious should fear wit is natural, the virtuous shun it, perhaps, because the possessors so often abuse and pervert it. Warburton, whose commentary was published in 1744, thus explains **by knaves undone :** " The poet would insinuate a common but shameful truth, that men in power, if they got power by illiberal acts, generally left wit and science to starve."

509. Commence its foe : begin to be its foe — the intransitive use.

511 Such . . . who : cf. note to l. 15.

514. The repetition of **crown** is an instance of carelessness rarely found in Pope.

519. Ill author . author is not one of the few words with which ill is used attributively The phrase is not idiomatic. We can say ' ill health,' ' ill nature,' ' ill wind,' etc. With other words *ill* is used predicatively — then the meaning changes, *i e.* ' the author is ill.'

521. Sacred . with the meaning *accursed,* imitates the Latin use.

528. Provoke : also with Latin force, meaning to call forth. Cf. Gray's *Elegy,* l 43.

534. In Roscommon's *Essay on Translated Verse* (l. 319) are words to the same effect.

> " Immodest words admit of no defense,
> For want of decency is want of sense."

Roscommon acted on this principle ; Pope's practice was far below his preaching. **The fat age of pleasure :** the reign of Charles II., the **easy monarch** referred to in l. 536.

538. The **jilts** were the mistresses of Charles II. See Green's *Short History of England*, p. 617, and Macaulay's *Essay on Milton*, edited by S. Thurber, p. 45. The statesmen who wrote farces were George Villiers, author of the *Rehearsal*, and Sir George Etherege, author of the *Man of Mode* and *She Would if She Could.*

539. Not all the wits had pensions. Butler, author of *Hudibras*, died in poverty; Otway died while hiding from his creditors; and Wycherley was left seven years in Fleet prison for debt. Dryden, laureate for Charles II., was long in indigence, and bitterly complained, "'Tis enough for one age to have neglected Mr. Cowley and starved Mr. Butler."

541. The reference is to the fashion among ladies of wearing masks at a play. Cibber attributes the custom to the gross immorality and indecency in the dramas of the day.

544. Foreign reign: *i.e.* that of William III. Originally the following couplet appeared here : —

> " There first the Belgian morals were extolled,
> We their religion had, and they our gold."

When these lines were taken out, Pope said that they contained "a national reflection which in his stricter judgment he could not but disapprove on any people whatever."

545 **Socinus** (1539-1604) : he opposed evangelical theology and denied the divinity of Christ, the doctrines of atonement, of original sin, of eternal punishment, of the personality of the Holy Spirit, and of the existence of Satan.

546. The **unbelieving priests** were the Latitudinarian divines at the time of William III. They advocated the union of the dissenters with the established church on the basis of such doctrines as were accepted by both parties. Pope is supposed to have had Bishop Burnet in mind

550 Cf. *Moral Essays*, IV. 149, 150, and Pope's note on that passage.

551. Cf. l. 391, and Milton, *Paradise Lost*, I. 690, II. 277, 278. See also *Century Dictionary*, under 'admire.'

553. Licensed blasphemies· Pope probably refers to Toland, Tindal, and Collins, defenders of deism, who were prominent at the end of the seventeenth and early eighteenth century. Cf. *Dunciad*, II. 399.

557 Mistake . . . into vice: "Misrepresent an author in order to pervert his meaning into something vicious."

571. Critic . *i e* critique, criticism

585. Appius: was Dennis, so named because of his play *Appius and Virginia*. Cf. note on l. 270. Pope calls him "a furious old critic." The 'stare' was one of his characteristics The word **tremendous**, too, has its point, for it was a great favorite with Dennis. In the farce *Three Hours after Marriage*, written by Gay and Pope, Dennis is introduced, and named Sir Tremendous.

588. Tax: *i.e.* censure. Cf. Celia's words to Touchstone, *As You Like It*, Act I. sc. ii. l. 82.

591. At one time noblemen received from the English universities the degree of M A. without examination

592. With this rhyme, cf. 301–302.

593. See Johnson's remarks on the practice of dedications, in the *Life of Dryden*. Pope abandoned this servile custom, and instead secured a list of subscribers for his Homer — a far better financial venture and one that preserved his independence.

603. Jades: old nags. See Skeat's *Etymological Dictionary*.

606–609. The reference is probably to Wycherley, a writer of comedies, who, when an old man, continued to scribble verses which were submitted to Pope for revision. See Macaulay's *Essay on the Comic Dramatists of the Restoration*.

617 Dryden's Fables. were his last work. They were published in 1700, the year in which the poet died They consisted of paraphrases of several tales from Chaucer and three from Boccaccio. **Durfey** (1653–1723): an author of the lowest order. He wrote some thirty dramatic pieces and compiled six volumes of songs and satires. The tales to which reference is made here were *Tales, Tragical and Comical* (1704), and *Tales, Moral and Comical* (1706). See Addison's words in Durfey's behalf in the *Guardian*, No. 67, May 28, 1713

619. Garth . . . Dispensary· Sir Samuel Garth (1660–1718) was an eminent physician. The *Dispensary* is a mock heroic poem in six cantos dealing with a feud between the apothecaries and the college of physicians. The physicians proposed to prescribe and furnish medicine gratuitously for the poor, and to this the apothecaries were opposed. The poem was famous at that time and for long afterward. Charges of plagiarism have been many. It was said that Johnson wrote the greater part of Goldsmith's *Traveller*, that Addison did not write *Cato*, that Goethe wrote most of Schiller's *Wallen-stein*, that Pope stole the present essay from Wycherley ; and our own century contributes the Bacon-Shakespeare "controversy."

622. No place *is* so sacred *that* from such fops *it is* barred. Warton notes that this satire is taken literally from Boileau, *L'Art Poétique*, IV. ll. 53–56.

623. Before the great London fire, Paul's churchyard was headquarters for the booksellers, and not a few may still be found there.

625. Cf. *Dunciad*, III. l. 213 ff.

632. Proud to know : see Abbott's *Shakespearian Grammar*, sec. 356, p 256. Cf. l. 642.

636 In Pope's day, humanly and humanely were not distinguished.

648 The Mæonian Star : *i.e.* Homer, so called because Smyrna, one of the seven cities that claimed to be his birthplace, was the capital of Mæonia, another name for Lydia in Asia Minor.

652. Aristotle is said to have **conquered nature** by virtue of his having written his *Physics;* by his *Rhetoric* and *Poetics* he presides over wit. With this line compare lines 98 and 99, where Pope tells us that the critics of old derived their rules from observation of the poets.

662. The student can ascertain the force of the word **phlegm** by consulting Skeat's *Etymological Dictionary.*

663–664. It seems strange that a writer of Pope's accuracy would allow this couplet to stand. What he means is that Horace does not suffer more by the wrong translations of the wits than he does by the misquotation of the critics. What does he say ?

665. Dionysius : "of Halicarnassus" (*Pope*). He was the author of numerous critical writings, some of which are still extant. Born between 78 and 54 B.C. ; died 7 B C.

667. Petronius : died A.D. 66 , was author of the immoral romance *Satirican* and was in high favor at Nero's court.

669. Grave Quintilian (42–118 A.D.): was the author of a valuable book, *De Institutione Oratoria*, which has come down to us.

675 Longinus (213 ?–273 A D) · is the supposed author of what is probably the best treatise on criticism ever written. It has been used as a text-book by most of the best critics, and fully justifies the tribute made here by Pope.

686. Rome before Pope's time, was pronounced *room*. Cf. Shakespeare's use in *Julius Cæsar*, Act. I. sc. ii. l. 156, and Act. III.

sc. i. l. 289; also in *King John*, Act. III. sc i. l. 180. With this passage compare Hallam's *Introduction to the Literature of Europe*, Chap. I.

693. Erasmus (1467-1536): did much for the dissemination of culture and learning. See Green's *Short History of the English People*, p. 305 ff. He was the glory of the priesthood through his genius; he was its shame, because he exposed its vice and corruption. In his *Encomium Moriæ* he demolished the tottering system of the monks (l. 696).

697. Leo's golden days: Pope Leo X. (1475-1521), son of Lorenzo de Medici, was destined for the church from childhood. He became a cardinal at the age of eleven, and served as pope from 1513-1521. To secure money for completing the rebuilding of St. Peter's begun by his predecessor Julius II., he issued indulgences, thereby increasing the discontent which culminated in the Reformation. His pontificate was unsuccessful, but he was an enthusiastic patron of literature and the arts.

704. Raphael (1483-1520): is recognized as the prince of painters. **Vida**: Marco Girolama (1490-1566) was one of the most distinguished writers at the time of Leo X. At the Pope's suggestion he wrote an epic called the *Christi*. His didactic poem, the *Art of Poetry*, furnished Pope with material freely adapted in the present essay. The poem was written shortly before Vida's death, and is devoted mainly to the consideration of the rules of epic verse. As a result of Pope's praise, it was translated into English by Christopher Pitt. Vida was made Bishop of Alba, and at Alba he spent the last years of his life.

707-708. Cremona: was Vida's birthplace; and, according to Pope, ranks next to **Mantua**, Virgil's birthplace.

709. The reference is to the sack of Rome by the Constable Bourbon in 1527.

714. Boileau-Despreaux (1636-1711): after a short career as an advocate, he began in 1666 to write, and met with immediate success He was to the literature of France at that time what Dryden and Pope were in their eras to English. His odes are poor, but his satires and critical writings are excellent. *L'Art Poétique* is a poem in four cantos, and summarizes the precepts of poetic literature. It was translated into English by Soame, who with Dryden's help changed the French personalities to references to English men of letters.

723. The reference is to John Sheffield, Duke of Buckingham

(1649–1721), in whose *Essay on Poetry*, l. 724 may be found. Dryden and Dr. Garth also praised him highly.

725. Roscommon: Wentworth Dillon (1633–1684) ; translated the *Ars Poetica* and wrote an *Essay on Translated Verse*, the only poem in blank verse between the death of Milton and the end of the seventeenth century. He was the first to recognize the splendor of *Paradise Lost*. With Dryden's help he formed a design for an English Academy after the plan of the one in France. The scheme has found favor with many English writers — Swift, Prior, Tickell, De Foe, and Matthew Arnold. He protested against the current grossness of expression. Pope says of him : —

> "In all Charles' days
> Roscommon only boasts unspotted lays."

See Johnson's *Life of Roscommon.*

729. William **Walsh** (1663–1708) : was one of Pope's early friends. Dryden said, "he was the best critic of our nation ; " De Quincey called him "a sublime old blockhead." He is preserved from oblivion by the advice he gave Pope, — to aim at correctness as the only means by which he might excel his predecessors   Pope's tribute is a graceful acknowledgment to one who has befriended and encouraged him. "In the statements of a panegyric one does not expect the rigor of an affidavit."

739 ad fin   These lines bear a close resemblance to the conclusion of Boileau's *L'Art Poétique.*

THOMAS GRAY.

1716–1771.

THOMAS was the fifth of the twelve children of Philip Gray, a London scrivener. His mother was Dorothy Antrobus, who, at the time of her marriage, kept a milliner's shop in partnership with her sister Mary, in Cornhill; and here Thomas was born, December 26, 1716.

Philip Gray was a wealthy man, and by his business skill added something to a large inheritance from his father. He was, however, a brutal husband and negligent father, and the poet was indebted for his education to the loving care and untiring industry of his mother. Thomas was sent to Eton by an uncle, and later entered Peterhouse College, Cambridge. At Eton began his life-long friendship with Horace Walpole. Here, too, were Richard West and Thomas Ashton, and these four formed "a quadruple alliance of the warmest friendship." They were amiable, gentle boys, all far from strong, and united doubtless by a warm sympathy in one another's suffering.

"Gray never was a boy," writes Walpole. A pale, quiet, studious lad, careless of his health and enamoured of learning—such was Gray in his school days and college life. He was a student and moralist while other boys were cricket players and healthy animals. At twenty he wrote a Latin theme in seventy-three hexameter lines that describes the mood of man as one of hesitation between the things of heaven and the things of earth. The thoughts are borrowed from Horace and Pope, but the verses are melodious and foreshadow the moral and elegiac style of his maturer years. The dull heaviness that then characterized Cambridge already weighted his nervous genius. His hours "may be best explained by negatives"; one day is like every other, "they go round and round like the blind horse in a mill, only he has the satisfaction of fancying he makes a progress; my eyes are open enough to see the same dull prospect and to know that having made four and twenty steps more, I shall be just where I was." He complains of the course of study, rebels against the strict requirements in mathematics, and denounces the careless neglect of the classics. His ill health and his dissatisfaction with the mental attitude of the university induced a passive melancholy that later developed into a depression of spirits from which he was never after wholly free.

In 1738, Gray left Cambridge without taking his degree. At the invitation and expense of Walpole, Gray accompanied his friend in a tour of the continent. Two years and a half, the healthiest and probably the happiest of his life, were spent in France, Italy, and Switzerland. At Reggio the friends quarrelled and parted; Walpole takes the fault upon himself — "he was a boy and Gray not yet man enough to make due allowances." This interruption of their intimacy was short; their natures were too generous to cherish sulky animosity, and three years later they were reunited.

In November, 1741, shortly after Gray's return to England, his father died. Almost his last act had been to squander his money in building a country house at Wanstead, so that of his ample fortune no more was left than by strict economy would provide for Mrs. Gray and her sisters. Gray therefore gave up his intended study of the law, and settled in Cambridge, where, except for two years spent in London at the time (1759) the British Museum was opened to the public, he made his home for the rest of his life. He lived in retirement, devoting all his masterful energy to scholarly attainments. Frequent visits to his mother at Stoke Pogis, to Mason at York, and Wharton at Durham, and a trip into Scotland varied the quiet regularity of his life. In 1753 his mother died. On her tombstone is an inscription, written by Gray, that bears witness to his love for the mother to whom he owed so much, — "the careful tender mother of many children, one of whom alone had the misfortune to survive her." The poet's health, never good, compelled him to forego a projected trip to Switzerland in the spring of 1771. He failed gradually, and an acute attack of the gout ended his life, July 30th of that year. He was buried, by his own request, beside his mother. Seven years later, on the 6th of August, — the anniversary of his funeral, — a monument, erected by Mason, was opened in Westminster Abbey. It is in the Poets' Corner, under the monument to Milton and next to that of Spenser; it is a medallion of Gray, and below, the inscription by Mason : —

> " No more the Grecian muse unrivalled reigns,
>   To Britain let the nations homage pay ;
>   She felt a Homer's fire in Milton's strains,
>   A Pindar's rapture in the lyre of Gray.
>
> He died July 30th, 1771. Aged 54."

Gray was a scholar. With the exception of Milton, no English poet had a broader or more accurate knowledge. He was a skilful linguist, a master of zoology and botany, thoroughly versed in the history of literature, and an enthusiastic student of architecture, music, and painting. Mathematics he ignored; but in nearly every other department of human learning he worked incessantly. When Greek was neglected, he studied it eagerly and left behind him a body of notes that attest his superiority of scholarship. His nervous fear of publicity and timorous dread of popularity made him a recluse. He rarely appeared among his fellow students at Cambridge; he even dined apart, and was seldom seen except on his trips to and from the college library. After Cibber died (1757), Gray was offered the laureateship, but declined the appointment. The following extract from a letter to his friend Mason shows us his opinion of the office and those who held it: " The office itself has always humbled the professor hitherto (even in an age when kings were somebody), if he were a poor writer by making him more conspicuous, and if he were a good one by setting him at war with the little fry of his own profession, for there are poets little enough to envy even a poet-laureate."

When we seek to discover Gray's influence over English poetry, we notice, first of all, that he produced very little. A few poems, numbering in all less than two thousand lines, include all his verse. In this small compass is the result of thirty years of study and meditation, — the bright, "fitful gleams of inspiration" that irradiated the melancholy solitude of his lonely life. Mr. Arnold says that Gray's sterility was caused by his living in the age of prose and reason: "the wells of poetry were stagnant, and there was no angel to strike the water." This condition had its influence on his temperament, no doubt, and possibly restrained him from freer expression. From another point of view, we may say that Gray was indifferent to the opinion of his contemporaries; that he had little respect for their learning, and never submitted himself to their judgment. A simple explanation of his lack of fertility lies near at hand. Gray was a scholar first, a poet afterward. He was devoted to research and critical investigation. Such a nature acquires much, but produces little. The time that other men spent in composition, Gray used in acquisition. When he did write, the mark of the careful scholar is on every line. "All his verses bear evidence of the most painstaking labor and rigorous self-criticism." Beside this limitation, we must remember that what creative power he did possess was held in check by wretched health throughout his life. The neglected body must restrict the activity of the intellect, however carefully that intellect may be cherished. And, last, he abhorred publicity. Even after he became the recognized chief of the writers of his day, no man was less familiar to the British public than England's greatest living poet. He wrote some sixty poems in English and Latin, but only twelve were published during his lifetime, and none of his prose appeared till after his death.

An examination of Gray's poetry reveals a steady progress toward romanticism. In his early verses he shows unmistakably the influence of Dryden and Pope. There is the same conventional moralizing, the same delight in personified abstractions, and the same trip-hammer regularity of rhythm that pleased the stilted ages of Anne and the Georges. There is little that foreshadows the Gray of the *Pindaric Odes* and the *Norse Fragments.* The three odes, *On the Spring, On a Distant Prospect of Eton College,* and *To Adversity,* written in 1742, have nothing of the spirit of romanticism, and "might have been written by any Augustan of sufficient talent." These compositions, with two didactic fragments, *De Principiis Cogitandi* and *On the Alliance of Education and Government*, constitute the work of Gray's first poetic period. The *Elegy*, which may be taken as representative of his second period, is not, indeed, purely romantic, though it differs widely from his earlier work. He had not yet freed himself from moralizing, and this was the quality which recommended the poem to Gray's contemporaries. What has rendered it immortal is its absolute perfection of language, — a beauty that his own age recognized but slowly. It has, too, a faultless evolution. Every line and each word has its own office. Not one could be altered without changing the thought. Here he first broke away from the cold laws of classicism (see note on line 60 of the *Elegy*). There are fewer personifications, more natural touches, and a recognition of English examples as sufficient to point the moral of his song. In the evolution of Gray's style, no one fact is of greater significance than his use of the names Hampden, Milton, and Cromwell in this poem. The spirit of nationalism triumphed over the Augustan adoration of Greece and Rome.

In the Pindaric odes (*Progress of Poesy*, 1754, and *The Bard*, 1757), Gray struck out in advance of his age, and helped to change its literary taste. The odes were not popular; people could not understand them, and, for that reason, ridiculed their obscurity. Their warmth could not thaw the ice of eighteenth-century formality. They are romantic in theme, stirring in treatment, perfect in form. The public was dazzled, and denied a beauty that in its blindness it could not see.

Gray's third period owes its inspiration to Mallett's *Introduction to the History of Denmark*, published in 1755. This volume had a profound influence on the changing spirit of the poet, and stirred him to an enthusiastic study of Norse mythology. Here was a field rich in romantic themes, and Gray's appreciation is seen in *The Fatal Sisters* (1761), *The Descent of Odin* (1764), and *The Triumphs of Owen* (1764). They are lyrics, pure and simple, "swallow-flights of song." In his *Observations on English Metre*, written probably in 1760–61, though first published in 1814, occurs a passage which clearly indicates his feeling toward the end of his life. "The more we attend to the composition of Milton's harmony," he writes, "the more we shall be sensible how he loved to vary his pauses, his measures, and his feet, which gives that enchanting air of freedom and wildness to his versification, unconfined by any rules but those which his own feeling and the nature of his subject demands."

Gray's merits as a poet consist in part in a musical sweetness of versification and a singular felicity of expression. Greater than these, perhaps, is his perfect art. "Gray," says Matthew Arnold, "holds his high rank as a poet not merely by the grace and beauty of passages in his poems; not merely by a diction generally pure in an age of impure diction: he holds it, above all, by the power and skill with which the evolution of his poems is conducted." They do not end, as is often the case with minor poets, simply because all poems must have an end somewhere, but because his theme is complete. In all, there is an evident plan, a growth of thought, a subordination of the less to the more essential part, and a clear relation between the beginning and the end. His greatest defects are an excess of allegory, something too much rhetoric, and personification so vague that Coleridge says, "it depends wholly on the compositor's putting or not putting a capital, whether the words should be personifications or mere abstracts." His merits are his own; his defects were due to his age as much as to himself. To Gray and Goldsmith, prophets of the new spirit in poetry, we owe much for what they did; still more, perhaps, for the inspiration they furnished to the poets who came after them.

ELEGY WRITTEN IN A COUNTRY CHURCHYARD.

It is very generally agreed that the *Elegy* was begun in 1742, finished in 1750, and then circulated privately among a few friends of the poet. Early in 1751, Gray received a letter from the editors of the *Magazine of Magazines*, an inferior periodical, asking permission to publish the poem. This request Gray was unwilling to grant, and on February 11th wrote to his friend Walpole and requested him to have Dodsley, the London printer, publish the *Elegy* at once. Walpole lost no time, and on February 28th the poem was issued anonymously in a quarto pamphlet, with the following prefatory advertisement: "The following poem came into my hands by accident, if the general approbation with which this little piece has been spread may be called by so slight a term as accident. It is this approbation which makes it unnecessary for me to make any apology but to the author: as he cannot but feel some satisfaction in having pleased so many readers already, I flatter myself he will forgive my communicating that pleasure to many more."

The poem was immediately reproduced in the magazines, and received a popular favor unsurpassed by any English composition. This popularity has continued until the present. Edition has followed edition in rapid succession; it has been translated into many foreign languages, living and dead; and, perhaps the surest evidence of favor, it has been frequently parodied. Conjectures as to the causes that inspired the poem and interesting facts concerning its publication may be found in Gosse's *Life of Gray*, pp. 66, 96.

1. Gray quotes from Dante, *Purgatory*, Canto VIII. See translations by Longfellow or Cary, opening lines of this canto. The word **curfew** occurs frequently in Shakespeare and at least twice in Milton, *Il Penseroso*, l. 74, and *Comus*, l. 435. For a description of the custom referred to, see Chamber's *Encyclopædia*, Vol III. p. 621, or Montgomery's *Leading Facts of English History*, p. 86.

2. Wind. is sometimes written 'winds' Which is better? Why? The student should read Collin's *Ode to Evening*. While there are few verbal similarities between it and the *Elegy*, the tones of the poems are so similar that comparison may be made profitable With reference to this line, note especially stanza X.

7. Cf. *Macbeth*, Act III. sc. ii.; *Ode to Evening*, stanza III.; and *Lycidas*, l. 28

13. "The yew-tree under which Gray often sat in Stoke churchyard still exists there; it is on the south side of the church, its branches spread over a large circumference, and under it, as well as under its shade, there are several graves." (Bradshaw's edition of *Gray's Works*, p. 215.)

16. Rude forefathers 'rude' refers to their rustic simplicity. It should be remembered that throughout the poem Gray has in mind the poor. They were buried outside the church; the rich inside. This custom prevailed in Gray's time and long before, but has since been abandoned This stanza and the ninth form the inscription on Gray's monument in Stoke Park.

20. Lowly bed: these words have by some editors been understood to refer to the grave. It seems much better, however, to take the expression literally.

21. Wakefield quotes Thomson, *Winter*, l. 311 ff., a passage of marked similarity in thought and in expression.

22. Ply her evening care: annotators have objected to this phrase. "To ply a care," Mitford says, "is an expression not proper to our language"; and Hales remarks : "This was probably the kind of phrase which led Wordsworth to pronounce the language of the *Elegy* unintelligible." Ply is a shortened form of apply, and is used by Milton as Gray uses it here. See *Paradise Lost*, IV. l. 264; also Thomson, *Winter*, l. 114. Whether the phrase be good or bad, it is the kind of diction against which Wordsworth so vigorously protested. When he had occasion to describe a similar scene, he wrote : —

> "And she I cherished, *turned her wheel*
> Beside an English fire."

26. Broke. see Abbott's *Shakespearian Grammar*, p. 343.

27. Drive their team afield: in *Lycidas*, l. 27, is a phrase almost identical with this. Milton's influence is easily recognized in Gray's poetry. The study of the lyrics should enable the student to discover for himself many interesting parallels. A few are indicated ; a little investigation on the part of the class will bring to light many more.

29. This stanza was used by Burns as a motto for his *Cotter's Saturday Night*. As has often been pointed out, the rhymes are poor, despite which the last line is perhaps the most famous in the whole range of English verse.

33. Wolfe, when sailing down the St. Lawrence on the night he attacked Quebec, is said to have repeated this poem to his brother officers When he had finished, he said, "I would rather be the author of that poem than take Quebec." How often must these words have recurred to his hearers as a pathetic prophecy of Wolfe's untimely end. Cf. note on l. 16. Mitford suggests that Gray may have had in mind the following verses from *Monody on Queen Caroline*, by his friend Richard West : —

> " Ah me ! what boots us all our boasted power,
>   Our golden treasure, and our purple state?
>   They cannot ward the inevitable hour,
>   Nor stay the fearful violence of fate."

35. Awaits: Mitford and Mason read "await," thinking that the subject was "the boast of heraldry," etc. Awaits is the form in Gray's manuscript and in all editions corrected by him. The inversion, too, is very common in Gray.

36. Hayley (*Life of Crashaw*, in *Biographia Britannica*) says that this line is "literally translated from the Latin prose of Bartholinus in his *Danish Antiquities.*"

43. Provoke. is used in its Latin sense. Mitford says "This use is unusually bold, to say the least." Cf. Pope, *Essay on Criticism*, l 528 and note.

51. "**Rage** is often used in the post-Elizabethan writers of the seventeenth century, and in the eighteenth century writers, for inspiration, enthusiasm." (*Hales.*)

53-56. This stanza has been furnished with many " originals." The thought is old, and had been many times expressed before Gray fixed for it an unchangeable form In Churchill's *Gotham* (II. l. 19), published in 1764, line 56 of the *Elegy* is quoted. This fact suggests that by that time the line, now so well known, had become a familiar quotation. Those who wish to compare expressions should look up Hall's *Contemplations*, VI. 872 ; Young's *Universal Passion*, V. ; Pope, *Rape of the Lock*, IV. l. 158 ; Waller's song, *Go, Lovely Rose*, etc. See also Gray's *Ode at the Installation*, ll. 71–76

57. John Hampden lived in Buckinghamshire, the county that contains the churchyard made immortal by this poem. He was a cousin of Oliver Cromwell, and in 1636 refused to pay the ship-money tax levied by Charles I. without the authority of Parliament. It will be noticed that Gray praises Hampden more than Cromwell, who was still very generally misunderstood.

59. Milton finished *Paradise Lost* at a cottage in the village of Chalfont St Giles, a few miles from Stoke Pogis. Look over your Macaulay's *Milton.*

60. "The prejudice against Cromwell was extremely strong through-

out the eighteenth century, even amongst the more liberal minded. . . .
His wise statesmanship, his unceasing earnestness, his high-minded
purpose, were not yet seen." (*Hales.*)

This stanza is important as an illustration of Gray's transition from
the classic to the romantic. The *Elegy* stands between his period of
classicism and his more imaginative poetry. Originally this stanza
read · —

> "Some village Cato, with dauntless breast
> The little tyrant of his fields withstood;
> Some mute inglorious Tully here may rest;
> Some Cæsar, guiltless of his country's blood."

The change from the Latin names to those of comparatively recent
history is full of significance. The spirit of nationalism has entered.
English heroes are good enough for English readers. Trifling as it
may appear to us now, Gray's desertion of classic names was a bold
movement that carried him a long distance in the right direction.

72 Here originally were inserted the following four stanzas : —

> "The thoughtless world to majesty may bow,
> Exalt the brave and idolize success;
> But more to innocence their safety owe,
> Than power or genius e'er conspired to bless.

> "And thou, who mindful of the unhonored dead,
> Dost in these notes their artless tale relate,
> By night and lonely contemplation led
> To wander in the gloomy walks of fate .

> "Hark ! how the sacred calm that breathes around,
> Bids every fierce tumultuous passion cease;
> In still, small accents whispering from the ground,
> A grateful earnest of eternal peace.

> "No more with reason and thyself at strife
> Give anxious cares and endless wishes room;
> But through the cool sequestered vale of life
> Pursue the silent tenor of thy doom."

Mason considers the third of these rejected stanzas equal to any in the
whole *Elegy.*

73. Far from the madding crowd: has been adopted as the title of a novel by Thomas Hardy. So also the *Annals of the Poor* (l. 32) is the title of Leigh Richmond's well-known work. 'Maddening' would be a more correct formation, but Gray's use of the word 'madding' has given it currency.

81. Epitaphs are famous for their ridiculous blunders. Under the yew-tree, in whose shade Gray wrote this poem, is a tombstone with ill-shaped letters and several words incorrectly spelled. In the inscription that Gray composed for his aunt's tomb, the word 'resurrection' is wrongly spelled.

85-88. This stanza is ambiguous. We may take **prey** in apposition with **who** or with **being**. Which is better?

90. Cf Pope, *Elegy on an Unfortunate Lady*, l. 49 ff.

89-92 This stanza gives a poetic answer to the question proposed in the preceding lines. Gray, in a note, quotes from Petrarch, Sonnet 169. Nott's translation is as follows : —

> "These, my sweet fair, so warns prophetic thought,
>   (Closed thy bright eye, and mute thy poet's tongue)
>   E'en after death shall still with sparks be fraught."

Line 92 closely resembles one in Chaucer, *Reeve's Prologue*, l. 3880. "It has been suggested that the first line of this stanza seems to regard the near approach of death ; the second, its actual advent ; the third, the time immediately succeeding its advent ; the fourth, a time still later." (Bradshaw, *Gray's Poetical Works*, p. 225.)

93-96. It will be observed that this stanza is the second of the rejected stanzas quoted above, slightly altered. Originally the following stanza was inserted · —

> "If chance that e'er some pensive spirit more
>   By sympathetic musings here delayed,
>   With vain though kind inquiry shall explore
>   Thy once loved haunt, this long-deserted shade."

98 Peep of dawn: cf. *Comus*, ll. 138–142, and Gray's *Installation Ode*, ll 30, 31.

100. Lawn: in Milton and Gray indicates nothing artificial, but means 'a cleared place in a wood.' See *Lycidas*, ll. 25–27 ; also

Deserted Village, l. 35. After this stanza, originally appeared the following : —

> "Him have we seen the greenwood side along,
>   While o'er the heath we hied, our labor done,
> Oft as the woodlark piped his farewell song,
>   With wistful eyes pursue the setting sun."

Mason wonders "that he rejected this stanza, as it not only has the same sort of Doric delicacy which charms us peculiarly in this part of the poem, but also completes the account of the whole song."

105-112. These two stanzas are inscribed on the monument to Gray in Stoke Park

115. For thou can'st read: the ability to read could not be taken for granted ; it was an accomplishment not much more common than good reading is to-day Bradshaw understands the clause as a poetical turn which by its repetition adds vividness to the old swain's speech.

116. After this stanza Gray originally had : —

> "There scattered oft, the earliest of the year,
>   By hands unseen are showers of violets found ;
> The redbreast loves to build and warble there,
>   And little footsteps lightly press the ground."

What reason can you suggest for omitting this quatrain, which Lowell says "cannot be obliterated from the memory of men, even if Gray did run his pen through it " ?

119. Science : is here a general term for knowledge.

THE PROGRESS OF POESY.

This ode was written at Cambridge, in 1754, but was not printed till 1757, when with the *Bard* it was issued from the press of Horace Walpole at Strawberry Hill, with the title. "*Odes by Mr. Gray*, printed at Strawberry Hill, for R. & J. Dodsley in Pall Mall. MDCCLVII." Walpole, writing to Sir Horace Mann, describes the odes as "amazing," "Shakespearian," "Pindaric," "sublime," and "consequently," he adds, "I fear a little obscure." So the public found them. In a later edition (1768) Gray added

explanatory notes, stating very frankly in a sarcastic advertisement
why he did so. "When the author first published this and the
following ode, he was advised even by his friends to subjoin some
few explanatory notes; but had too much respect for the understanding of his readers to take that liberty." The part of Gray's
notes that could assist the student are given below; those that tend
to confuse him are omitted.

The English Pindaric Ode.

In Gray's day the ode had long held a place in English literature. Ben Jonson wrote an ode, divided, as Pindar's were, into
strophe, antistrophe, and epode, terms derived from the movements
of the Greek chorus. These parts Jonson called respectively the
turn, counterturn, and stand. Cowley's Pindaric odes appeared
in 1656. These, however, were not imitations of the Greek poet,
but shapeless products of the Englishman's fancy. His stanzas
are verse groups of irregular length, ending with a long line, and
he thought that his variations made his compositions Pindaric.
The complexity of Pindar's metre was mistaken for lawlessness.
The measure gained favor rapidly and became the favorite form
for poet-laureates. Shapelessness was indeed well suited to their
vapid utterance. Congreve "cured the Pindaric madness." In
1706 he published a Pindaric entirely correct in form. The preface is a *Discourse on the Pindaric Ode*, in which he said. "The
character of these late Pindarics is a bundle of rambling, inco-
herent thoughts, expressed in a like parcel of irregular stanzas. . . .
On the contrary, there is nothing more regular than the odes of
Pindar." Gray was the most famous writer of Pindarics after
Cowley and Congreve; his *Progress of Poesy* and *Bard* are the
best English poems in this form.

As is indicated in the text, the *Progress of Poesy* is divided into
three stanzas of forty-one lines each. Each stanza is again divided
into the three parts, — strophe, antistrophe, and epode. The three
strophes, antistrophes, and epodes are identical in structure, and
the whole poem, therefore, is absolutely symmetrical, and a correct
imitation of the Greek odes.

The motto is from Pindar, *Olymp.* II. ll. 153, 154. Gray, in a letter (1763) to Rev. James Brown, writes. "The odes, . . . as their motto shows, were meant to be *vocal to the intelligent alone.* How far they were, in my own country, Mr. Howe can testify; and yet my ambition was terminated by that small circle." A writer in the *Critical Review* suggested that the author might have added : —

ἐς
Δὲ τὸ πᾶν ἐρμενέων χατίζει.

"For the many there is need of an interpreter."

In the edition of 1768 the suggestion was adopted.

1. Gray quotes *Psalms*, lvii 8, "Awake, my glory, awake, lute and harp." What is his inaccuracy? **Æolian lyre** was mistaken by the *Critical Review* for the harp of Æolus, or wind-harp. Gray added this note, "Pindar styles his own poetry with its musical accompaniments, Æolian song, Æolian strings, the breath of the Æolian flute."

1–12. "The subject and simile, as usual with Pindar, are united. The various sources of poetry . . . are here described." (*Gray.*)

3. Helicon's harmonious springs two springs, Hippocrene and Aganippe, sacred to the Muses, were in the Helicon range of mountains in Bœotia.

7. Cf. Thomson, *Liberty*, II. l. 256 ff. ; Pope, *Ode on St. Cecilia's Day*, l. 11.

10. Amain: means literally with force ; we still have the phrase 'with might and main.' Cf. Milton, *Lycidas,* l 111.

12 Rebellow. is imitated from the Latin *reboare*. Rolfe quotes Pope, *Iliad*, "Rocks rebellow to the roar"

13–24. "Power of harmony to calm the turbulent sallies of the soul. The thoughts are borrowed from the first Pythian of Pindar." (*Gray.*)

14. Cf. Comus, l 555.

15 Enchanting shell: *i.e.* the lyre. The allusion is to the myth that Hermes made the instrument from the shell of a tortoise.

17. Thrace was one of the chief seats of the worship of Mars, **the Lord of War.**

20. "This is a weak imitation of some incomparable lines in the same ode" (the first Pythian of Pindar). (*Gray.*)

25-41. "Power of harmony to produce all the graces of motion in the body." (*Gray.*)

27. Idalia was a town in Cyprus, and contained a temple sacred to Venus Pope uses the same form in his *First Pastoral*, l. 65. Dr. Johnson objects to the compound **velvet-green** on the ground that nature should not borrow from art. See his *Life of Gray.*

29. Cytherea: a name for Venus. It was derived from Cytherea, an island in the Ægean, where many believed she had landed before she appeared on Cyprus.

30. Antic and antique are the same Cf. Milton, *Il Penseroso*, l. 158.

31. Frolic: is here used as an adjective. Milton has the word at least twice in the same usage. Cf. *Comus*, l. 59, and *L'Allegro*, l. 18. The rhythm of this line is suggestive of *L'Allegro*.

35. Gray quotes *Odyssey*, VIII. l. 265. "He gazed with delight at the quick twinkling of the dancer's feet and was astonished at heart." Cf. Thomson, *Spring*, l. 158.

40-41. Gray's verse shows, as was pointed out in the sketch of his life, a gradual change from classicism to romanticism. But few of his lines show so warm a feeling as is here evinced, though this would be cold for Tennyson. Gray quotes from the tragic poet Phrynicus. A free translation is, "The light of love shines in her rosy cheeks."

42-53. "To compensate the real and imaginary ills of life, the muse was given to mankind by the same Providence that sends the day by its cheerful presence to dispel the gloom and terrors of the night." (*Gray.*)

43 ff. The personification of abstractions was one characteristic of the classic school of writers. These lines furnish the most striking illustration, in this poem, of Gray's fondness for this quality. Cf. the odes on *Spring, Death of a Favorite Cat, Eton College*, and the *Hymn to Adversity.*

50 Birds of boding cry: called, in colloquial speech, screech-owls.

52. The variations of lines 52 and 53 found in the manuscripts are given to show the care with which Gray's verses were written : —

"Till fierce Hyperion from afar
    Pours on their scattered rear ⎫
    Hurls at   "   flying   "   ⎪ his glittering shafts
      " o'er " scattered " ⎬   of war.
      "   "   " shadowy " ⎭
    Till   "   "   "   "   from far
    Hyperion hurls around," etc.

Hyperion, *i.e.* the sun, was a Titan, the father of the sun, moon, and stars   Cf. Lowell, *Vision of Sir Launfal*, l. 132 ff.   Gray's note quotes inaccurately from Cowley's Pindaric ode, *Brutus*, ll. 55–57 : —

    " Or seen the morning's well-appointed star
    Come marching up the eastern hills afar."
                            — Cowley.

54-65. " Extensive influence of poetic genius over the remotest and most uncivilized nations, its connection with liberty, and the virtues that naturally attend on it.   (See the Erse, Norwegian, and Welsh fragments, the Lapland and American songs.)"   (*Gray.*)   **Solar road** : the figure is a favorite with poets   See Virgil, *Æneid*, VI. l. 795 ; Dryden, *Annus Mirabilis*, stanza 160 ; *Threnodia Augustalis*, l. 353 ; and Pope, *Essay on Man*, I. l 102.

64. Rolfe quotes from Dugald Stewart, *Philosophy of the Human Mind*, " I cannot help remarking the effect of the solemn and uniform flow of verse in this exquisite stanza, in retarding the pronunciation of the reader, so as to arrest his attention to every successive picture, till it has time to produce its proper impression."

66-82 " Progress of poetry from Greece to Italy and from Italy to England."   (*Gray.*)

68   **Ilissus** : is a river that flows through Athens.

69.   **Mæander** : see etymology of the verb ' meander.'

70.   Cf. *Comus*, l. 232

82.   Poetry is at its best in times of national progress and of greatest freedom.   When Greece was conquered, poetry went to Rome ; and when Rome fell, to England.

84. Nature's darling : " Shakespeare "   (*Gray.*)   Shakespeare is called a child of nature because he had little knowledge of Greek and Latin, the recognized learning of the sixteenth and seventeenth centuries. See Ben Jonson's lines *To the Memory of Shakespeare*, and Milton's *L'Allegro*, l. 132 ff.

86. The mighty mother: may be either nature or poetry.

89. Pencil. the etymology of this word will show its meaning here.

91. Golden keys: cf. *Comus*, l. 12, and *Lycidas*, l. 110.

95. Nor second he "Milton." (*Gray.*) In a letter to Richard Hurd, Gray wrote: "I have heard of nobody but a player and a doctor of divinity that profess their esteem for them [*i.e.* Gray's *Pindarics*]. Oh, yes! a lady of quality who is a great reader. She knew there was a compliment to Dryden, but never suspected there was anything said about Shakespeare or Milton till it was explained to her, and wishes there had been titles prefixed to tell what they were about."

99. Gray quotes (inaccurately) from *Ezekiel*, Chap. i. 20, 26, and 28

102. Gray quotes from *Odyssey*, VIII. l. 64. "(Though) deprived of sight, he gave sweet song" See Dr. Johnson's comment in *Life of Gray*

103. It is worthy of note that Gray places Shakespeare and Milton before Dryden, though he once advised Beattie to study Dryden, saying that "if there was any excellence in his own numbers, he had learned it wholly from that great poet." At the time when the *Progress of Poesy* was written, Gray, like others whose romanticism was more pronounced, had given himself up to a veneration for Milton. His debt to Dryden was never forgotten. In 1765 he wrote to Beattie: "Remember Dryden, and be blind to his faults."

106. "Meant to express the stately march and sounding energy of Dryden's rhymes." (*Gray.*) Cf. Pope, *Imitations from Horace*, Ep. II l. 267 ff.

109. Pictured urn: *i.e.* urn with pictures on it. Cf Milton, *Il Penseroso*, l. 159, and Gray, *Elegy*. l 41.

111. "We have had in our language no other odes of the sublime kind than that of Dryden on *St. Cecilia's Day;* for Cowley (who had his merit) yet wanted judgment, style, and harmony for such a task. That of Pope is not worthy of so great a man. Mr. Mason, indeed, of late days, has touched the true chords, and with a masterly hand, in some of his choruses; above all, in the last of *Caractacus:* —

"'Hark! heard ye not yon footstep dread!' etc." (*Gray.*)

I

115. After quoting from Pindar, *Olymp.* II. l. 159, Gray adds, "Pindar compares himself to that bird and his enemies to the ravens that croak and clamor in vain below, while it pursues its flight, regardless of their noise."

121–123. These lines show Gray's own character and his poetic aim , at the same time there is a suggestion of the modesty that kept him in a secluded life.

OLIVER GOLDSMITH.

1728-1774.

THE year 1728 witnessed several events of importance in the history of English literature. Thomson published his *Spring*, Gay brought out the *Beggar's Opera*, and Pope sent forth the *Dunciad*. In this year was born Thomas Percy, who rescued from oblivion so many of our old English ballads; and on the 10th of November, Oliver Goldsmith was born at Pallas, County Longford, Ireland. Two years later, his father, a clergyman of the Established Church, secured a better living at Lissoy, and the Goldsmith family moved thither. Oliver's school-days were spent in idleness. At Trinity College (1744-1749) he did not mend his ways, and during the two years that followed his graduation he was contentedly dependent on the industry of his mother and the generosity of his friends. He made lazy attempts to teach, to take orders, to study law, and once set forth with half-hearted determination to make his fortune in America. He lacked the force of character that would have enabled him to fix a definite purpose and carry it out. All his plans were visionary; he failed in everything he undertook. His uncle Contarine finally furnished the improvident youth with money to start him in medical study at Edinburgh.

For eighteen months Goldsmith studied, or pretended to study, at this university, and then, following one of his many restless impulses, rambled away on his famous European tour, with the ostensible purpose of continuing his study of medicine. Perhaps he did study some, though the only evidence for such assumption is the mention of Albinus and Glaubius, famous men at Leyden, in letters to the over-credulous uncle Contarine. It is more probable that the time was passed in idling or gambling — vices which

had always no small attraction for susceptible Goldsmith. He
stayed at Leyden but a short time, and then, with but a guinea in
his pocket, started upon his vagrant trip through the Continent.

Little is known, though much has been conjectured, about this
period of Goldsmith's life. Legend has it that he paid his way by
performances on the flute, and many interesting stories have been
based on the narrative of the philosophic vagabond in the *Vicar of
Wakefield*. Boswell, Johnson's chattering biographer, tells us that
the wanderer "disputed" his way through Europe. It seems more
probable that he begged his way — an assumption that is justified
by Goldsmith's custom both before and after this time. Somewhere the vagrant picked up a medical degree, but how and where
has never been related.

On his return to London, in 1756, Goldsmith began his struggle
for life. He had no money, no friends, and but few acquaintances.
Even his appearance was against him, and his awkward presence
and ugly face doubtless brought him many rebuffs. At length he
secured employment in a chemist's shop, and later became a press-
corrector for Samuel Richardson.

While at Edinburgh, Goldsmith had been a fellow-student with
a son of the Dr. Milner who kept a boys' school at Peckham. By
the influence of this friend the press-corrector secured an appointment as usher. Dr. Milner's daughter tells us that "this Irish
usher of theirs was a remarkably cheerful and even facetious per-
son, constantly playing tricks and practical jokes, amusing the
boys by telling stories and by performances on the flute, living a
careless life, and always in advance of his salary." By the Mil-
ners, Goldsmith was introduced to Mr. Griffith, proprietor of *The
Monthly Review*, who offered him board and lodging and a liberal
salary to write articles of a critical nature for the magazine.
Goldsmith closed with the offer, and thus began the hack-writing
which for the rest of his life continued to be his vocation. He
quarrelled with Griffith, as indeed he did with most of his employ-
ers, but the publishers of the day furnished him with all that he
could do. Usually payment was made in advance, and the money
was frequently spent long before the work was completed. He
never lived within his income, and his efforts were always directed

toward paying up arrears. The work compiled under these circumstances was widely varied, — a miscellaneous product of pamphlets, tracts, abridgments, essays, sketches, — in short, anything of a marketable nature. *The Bee, The Citizen of the World, Histories of England, Rome,* and *Greece,* a *History of Animated Nature,* and the *Life of Beau Nash* were among his tasks. The work was done to order, but none the less possessed a vivacity that secured for his compilations a wide popularity. He was not a historian and no more a naturalist. This the histories themselves abundantly testify. But he did make interesting books; "he touched nothing he did not adorn." Johnson thought the *Natural History* would be as agreeable as a Persian tale. So indeed it is, and though the treatise has no value as a contribution to science, it shows the poet's sympathizing love for all that lives.

But Goldsmith's fame does not rest on his task work. At intervals he turned from his drudgery and added a classic to our literature. As an essayist, a novelist, a poet, and a playwright, his work entitles him to a place of honor in our literary history. In his contributions to *The Bee* and to *The Citizen of the World,* he was an imitator of Addison and of Steele. But he does not end in imitation. In the *Vicar of Wakefield,* the character essay is invested with a new charm. The sketches are united into a continuous plot. Goldsmith herein exemplifies a change that is significant in the literary history of his time. All that the *Sir Roger de Coverley Papers* lack of being a novel is the unified and heightened interest that belongs to a regularly constructed plot. This want Goldsmith supplied in the plan that correlates the characters of his prose-pastoral — a work that Carlyle called "the best of all modern idylls." In comedy he led the revolt against the affected sentimentalism then prevailing, and inaugurated a new era of the drama. It was with difficulty that Colman, the manager of Covent Garden Theatre, was persuaded to present *The Good-natured Man* and *She Stoops to Conquer,* fearing that the "vulgar humors" of the plays would shock the hypersensitive feelings of the theatre-goers of that age. In *The Traveller* and *The Deserted Village* Goldsmith is again ahead of his time. In form they are similar to that required by the fashion in the preceding age, but their spirit is essentially that of the new literary and social England. Gold-smith's position is anomalous; he belongs to neither the old nor the new school. The new spirit is disguised in a solemn garb of classic style. " He filled old bottles with new wine," not in a single department, but in all the varied forms of his compositions. He improved on his predecessors and made a high standard for those of later time.

Goldsmith, the man, was marked by many seeming contradictions in character. He earned sufficient money to pay his debts, to make himself comfortable, and, indeed, to obtain some few of life's luxuries. Had his earnings been twice as much as they were, he would doubtless have spent more than his income. Extravagance was a part of his nature. He was always improvident and never seemed able to realize the value of money. Experience taught him nothing; past folly was forgotten when the trouble it occasioned had gone. This weakness made his whole life one of embarrassment and disgrace. An oft-repeated anecdote of Johnson and Goldsmith is so characteristic of the poet that we give it here. Johnson one day received a letter from Goldsmith, imploring him to come at once to his relief. Johnson sent a guinea by the messenger and promised to follow as speedily as he could. When he arrived, he found that Goldsmith had been arrested by his landlady for arrears of rent. On the table stood a bottle of Madeira, for which a part of the guinea had been already exchanged. Goldsmith's clothes had been seized by his landlady, and the poet was in a towering passion. Johnson persuaded him to be calm and discuss the means by which he might be extricated. It was on this occasion that Johnson sold *The Vicar of Wakefield* for the sum of £60, with which the landlady's claims were satisfied, and Goldsmith was once again set free. Doubtless in the poet's life there were many similar episodes. Only the moment concerned him; to-morrow's needs always seemed the demands of a future too remote to deserve serious consideration. Forster, in his biography of Goldsmith, rates mankind roundly for a lack of appreciation in permitting this genius to importune the " draggle-tailed muses " so vainly. The criticism is unjust and foolish. Goldsmith was well paid for all he did; if he chose to squander his money and run in debt, the world was not to blame, nor should Goldsmith, more than other men, escape the consequences of folly. It is better to recognize his failing frankly. By so doing, we evince no lack of affection for the poet who contributed so much to the development of our literature. The possession of genius does not exempt a man from the obligation of paying his debts. Despite his laxity in financial matters, he was never in want of credit. "Was ever poet so trusted!" exclaimed Johnson, when told, after Goldsmith's death, that he had died £2000 in debt. The world had paid him this much more than he had earned. There is little excuse for the cry of ingratitude and inappreciation. Toward the end of his life, the embarrassments increased. More and more deeply he became involved in difficulties from which he could find no escape. They preyed on his spirits and undermined his health, till at last he fell sick. He doctored himself and would permit no physician to be called. His friends took alarm, but despite their protests he persisted in his obstinate course until it was too late for medical skill to be of any help. He died on the 4th of April, 1774.

Goldsmith was loved by all who knew him. Burke, when told of his death, burst into tears, and Reynolds put aside his brush. While the poet lay dying, the stairs leading to his chambers were thronged by wretched creatures whose distress his generous hand had often relieved when he himself was in sorer straits. There was in his character nothing selfish, nor sordid, nor mean. He was simple, genuine, unaffected; these qualities of his character shine in quiet beauty in the tender pathos, the quaint humor, the pure diction and grace of touch that mark all he wrote, and lend to even his hack-work a singular dignity. Johnson, who was long one of the poet's nearest friends, gives advice that we may well follow: "Let not his frailties be remembered: he was a very great man."

THE TRAVELLER.

This poem, dedicated to his brother, and the first to which Goldsmith signed his name, was published in December, 1764. It had been begun in 1755, while the poet was in Switzerland, but remained uncompleted until shortly before its publication. The success of the poem was immediate and unqualified; four editions were needed in eight months, and before the author's death five more were issued. Johnson wrote a favorable notice of the poem for the *Critical Review.* The members of the "Literary Club" could hardly credit the "newspaper essayist" and "literary drudge" with a poem of the elevated diction and the sound sense that characterize *The Traveller.* Goldsmith had been known as a stammering talker, plainly at a disadvantage with the skilled conversationalists who were his associates. *The Traveller* raised him at once to his proper place among his intellectual peers.

It is possible that a suggestion of this poem may have been made by Addison's *Letters from Italy.* The poet Thomson seems to have had in mind a poem similar in plan to *The Traveller.* In a letter to a friend, he wrote, "A poetical landscape of countries, mixed with moral observations on their character and people, would not be an ill-judged undertaking." It was reserved for Goldsmith to execute this plan in a manner peculiarly his own. To describe the poem as a poetic diary would be unjust; yet it is certain that the poet's personal observations during his European travel are presented with the sincerity of feeling that characterizes a generous, honest heart.

1. Slow: at a meeting of the club shortly after this poem appeared, one of the members asked Goldsmith if by 'slow' he meant tardiness of locomotion. "Yes," he replied; but Johnson caught him up, exclaiming, "No, sir, you did not mean tardiness of locomotion, you meant that sluggishness of mind which comes upon a man in solitude." "Ah, that was what I meant," returned Goldsmith. From this episode arose a suspicion that Johnson wrote the line, as well as many others; but Boswell's curiosity set the world right. Johnson, at his biographer's request, marked the lines which he contributed to *The Traveller*, and they will be indicated in the notes. Whichever meaning the poet had in mind, he chose the right word.

2 Scheldt and **Po**: these rivers mark the geographical limits of the travels described in the poem. The Scheldt flows north from France, through Belgium and Holland.

3. Cunningham wrote (1853), "Carinthia still retains its character for inhospitality." The province is in Austria and east of the Tyıol. Goldsmith's visit was made ın 1755.

5. Campania: Goldsmith undoubtedly refers to the Campagna, an unhealthful, malarious plain near Rome. The spelling in the text seems to be without any authority, and is misleading, from the fact that there is a province named Campanıa, south of the central part of Italy.

10. The thought of thıs lıne is expanded by Washington Irving, in *The Sketch-Book*, sketch called *The Voyage*. Goldsmith has the same thought ın *The Cıtızen of the World*, Letter III. It may be found also in Cibber's (1671–1757) *Commercial Lover*.

13-22 Cf. *Deserted Vıllage*, ll. 149–162, where thıs thought is more fully developed.

17. In the first edıtion this line reads . —

"Blest be those feasts where mirth and peace abound."

23. Me: is the object of the verb **leads**, l. 29.

27. The attention of the student is dırected to the combination of simile and metaphor in this passage. Comment on such arrangement may be found ın the rhetorics by A. S Hıll and J. D. Quackenbos.

32. I sit me down cf. *Deserled Vıllage*, l. 86. A sımılar use of 'sit' may be found ın *Love's Labor's Lost*, Act I. sc i ; in Tennyson's *Lotus Eaters*: —

"They sat them down upon the yellow sand,"

and in Milton, *Paradise Lost*, IX. l. 1121 Thıs reflexive use was common among the old writers and ıs ıecognized by both Webster and Worcester. Some grammarians give it as false syntax and would change 'sıt' to 'set.'

33. Cf. *Deserted Village*, ll. 188–190.

41. School-taught pride: ı.e. the prıde felt by him who has been taught in the schools of the philosophers, especially of the Stoıcs.

50. What is the construction of **heir**?

58. To see: thıs use of the infinitive is very common in Shake-speare, but ıs rarely found in modern wrıtıng See Abbott's *Shake-spearıan Grammar*, sec. 356. Cf. l. 62

69. Line: equator, as ın Tennyson's *Enoch Arden*, l. 601.

72. Why not 'give' instead of **gave**?

73. Cf. Cowper's *Task*, Bk. II. l. 206 ff.

84. Idra's cliff — Arno's shelvy side: Idra or Idria, rich in quicksilver mines, is in the duchy of Carniola, Austria. The Arno flows through a fertile part of Italy. There is therefore a means of livelihood in both sterile and productive places.

85. Frown: here means little more than 'are.' The emphatic idea of this line is in **rocky-crested**, and is contrasted with **beds of down** in the line following.

87. Art: is here used in its widest sense. In ll. 146 and 304, it means 'the fine arts.'

90. Hales suggests that the word **either** may be justified by supposing the blessings enumerated to be divided into two classes: (1) the one prevailing; (2) the others, which are cast into the shade by that prevailing one. Lines 91 and 92 are illustrations supporting the doubtful statements made in 89 and 90. Contentment does not necessarily 'fail' under wealth nor under freedom. In England commerce has long prevailed, but we do not consider English merchants, let alone the English nation, as a band of rogues devoid of honor. A certain amount of freedom creates a desire for more, and discontent arises, not from the freedom granted, but from that withheld. Read Macaulay on the ills produced by newly acquired freedom (*Essay on Milton*, p. 25, ed. by S. Thurber). See also Wordsworth's sonnet beginning —

"When I have borne in memory what has tamed."

101. Proper: own, in a kind of antithesis to 'mankind' in l. 102

108. "The stage often borrows similes and metaphors from nature; here nature is made indebted to the stage." (*Hales*) Cf. Milton's *Paradise Lost*, IV. l. 137 ff., and Virgil's *Æneid*, I. l. 164

111-112. The lines imply that nature's bounty cannot satisfy the breast, and that therefore the sons of Italy are not blessed. Latin grammars describe such conditional forms as contrary to fact in present time.

116 The varied year: the four seasons.

118. Vernal lives: lives no longer than the spring.

121 Gelid. the word is not poetic and is worthy of Dr. Johnson. The editor has failed to find the word in any other poet save Thomson, who uses it twice in *The Seasons*.

127. Manners: is used in the sense of the Latin *mores*, the custom or mode of life. Cf. *Deserted Village*, l. 74 ; Shakespeare, *Lucrece*, l. 1397 ; and Wordsworth, *Sonnet to Milton*.

129. Zealous : in a religious sense. It does not seem clear that poverty and gravity are faults, so much as they are misfortunes. These qualities, blameless in themselves, are here contrasted with positive vices.

134 When commerce proudly flourished : it was in the fifteenth century that the Italian republics, Venice, Genoa, Florence, and Pisa, were at the height of their prosperity.

136. Long-fallen · *i.e.* since the days of old Rome. The reference in this and the following lines is to the Italian renaissance in the fifteenth century. At this period of Italy's history, architecture, sculpture, and painting were at their zenith.

140. The Mediterranean was the means of communication between east and west until the sea route round the Cape of Good Hope was discovered by Magellan, 1497. This, and the discovery of America, were two main causes for the decline of Italian commerce.

143. Skill : is used in its older sense of ' knowledge.'

150. The pasteboard triumph : refers to the carnival mummeries, modern Italy's substitute for the real splendor of the old Roman triumphs.

153. Irving says that Sir Joshua Reynolds called upon Goldsmith one morning while he was engaged in the composition of this poem. The poet was sitting at his desk and engaged in the double occupation of writing *The Traveller* and teaching a pet dog to " sit up." At one moment he glanced his eye at his desk and the next shook his finger at the dog. " The last lines on the page were still wet ; they form part of the description of Italy.

> " ' By sports like these are all their cares beguiled,
> The sports of children satisfy the child.'

Goldsmith joined in the laugh caused by his whimsical enjoyment, and acknowledged that his boyish sport with the dog suggested the stanza."

159. Domes : is used in the poetic sense of mansion or palace. Cf. *Deserted Village*, l. 319, and Byron, *Childe Harold*, canto I. stanza XXIV.

167. Bleak Swiss their stormy mansion tread · bleak, applied to the Swiss, is one of the most striking instances of a figure frequently found in Goldsmith's writing. What is the figure? Find other instances. **Mansion**: is used in its literal (now obsolete) sense of an abiding place. Cf. Milton's *Comus*, l. 2; *Il Penseroso*, l. 93; *John*, xiv. 2.

170. Man and steel: must be taken together, and as explained by the rest of the line means armed troops. Goldsmith does not mean that steel is found in Switzerland's mountains. **The soldier and his sword**: from the middle of the seventeenth century Swiss mercenaries were employed throughout Europe, especially in France and Spain. Read Chap. VII. Bk. II. of Carlyle's *French Revolution*. Reed says, "In many of our old plays the guards attendant on kings are called Switzers, and that without any regard to the country where the scene lies." Cf. *Hamlet*, Act. IV. sc. v. l. 80.

174. With this suggestion of the power of a storm in the Alps, cf. Byron's *Childe Harold*, canto III.

176. Redress. here means to make amends for; cf. l. 214, where **redrest** means 'supplied.'

178. This line furnishes the reason for the content mentioned in l. 175 — there is nothing to excite envy.

186. Breasts: is the reading in all the early editions, and this line is quoted in Johnson's *Dictionary* to illustrate the verb. 'Breathes' is found in the Globe edition and a few others. A misprint seems to be the only reason for such change.

190. Savage: is rarely used as a noun except with reference to human beings. Cf. *Citizen of the World*, I., and *As You Like It*, Act II. sc. vi. l. 6.

194 Cf. Gray's *Elegy*, l. 21.

198. Nightly: means simply 'for the night,' instead of a series of nights, as usual. Shakespeare often has the word in this sense. In the petition, "Give us this day our daily bread," 'daily' has a similar use For a picture somewhat similar, cf. *Deserted Village*, ll. 155-160.

219, 220. Is the metaphor clear?

221 Level. means unvaried, monotonous.

232. Fall. is the form correct? How may it be defended?

234. Cowering: means brooding, and includes no idea of fear.

243. Perhaps some of Goldsmith's experiences were the basis for these lines. See *Vicar of Wakefield*, Chap. XX., "History of a Philosophic Vagabond"

253. Gestic lore: in Webster's *Dictionary* this line is quoted to

illustrate 'gestic' in the sense of "pertaining to feats of arms."
With such meaning the phrase becomes pointless. There is no pro-
priety in assigning skill in arms to the dancing grandsire, while there
is an eminent fitness in saying he was a good dancer. Scott uses the
word at least twice in this sense ; once in the *Abbot*, Chap. XXVII ,
where he describes Catherine Seyton as skilled in gestic lore ; and
again in *Peveril of the Peak*, Chap. XXX., where, describing Fenella's
performance before King Charles, he says that the king " seemed, like
herself, carried away by the enthusiasm of the gestic art." The
Standard Dictionary marks the word obsolete.

256. Thus idly busy rolls their world away: ' idly busy ' is
the rhetorical figure called oxymoron. Cf. Pope, *Elegy on an Unfortunate Lady*, l. 81 ; *Hamlet*, Act III. sc. ii. l. 253 ; *As You Like It.* Act
II. sc. vii. l. 23.

265, 266. Campbell, in *Specimens of the British Poets*, referring
to these two lines, says, " There is perhaps no couplet in English
rhyme more perspicuously condensed than those two lines of *The
Traveller* in which he describes the once flattering, vain, and unhappy
character of the French."

276. Frieze . is a coarse cloth brought originally from Friesland.

277. Cheer : here means good fare. The derivation of the word
should be noted.

286. Rampire : poetic for rampart, meaning the dikes.

297. Wave-subjected : the meaning here is not clear. Rolfe
explains it as " lying below the level of the waves." This explanation, however, furnishes no cause for the " repeated toil " mentioned
in the next line. If we take the passage to mean simply ' subject to
inundation,' we have a clear relation of cause and effect, and a meaning in accord with the context.

303. What is the subject of **are** ?

306. Even liberty itself, etc. : this may refer to the custom which
allowed a parent to sell his child's labor for a term of years. It is
possible that an allusion is here made to the support which the Repub-
licans, under the leadership of John and Cornelius De Witt, gave to
the French in the time of Louis XIV.

309 ff. Goldsmith's attack on the Dutch is in no way justifiable.
Many pages of their history must have been cut out before the book
came into the poet's hands. This is not the only instance (Vid.
Citizen of the World, Letter CXVIII.) in which he fails to show even

fairness to a hardy, industrious, heroic people. The debt of liberty, civil and religious, to the Netherlands cannot be unknown to the most casual reader Goldsmith perhaps forgot that England's prowess had more than once yielded to Dutch valor. The bravery of William of Orange and William de la Marck and the long commercial supremacy of the Dutch should have guarded them from such prejudiced aspersions.

310 Cf *Julius Cæsar*, Act. I. sc ii l. 135 ff.

318 Cf. *Citizen of the World*, Letter CXIV.

319. Lawns: cf. *Deserted Village*, l. 35 ; *Paradise Lost*, IV. l. 252 ; and *Citizen of the World*, Letter CXIV. Arcadia, situated in the Peloponnesus, now the Morea, was taken by the poets as typical of pastoral simplicity and beauty.

320. Hydaspes· is now called Jelum, a tributary to the Indus. Cf. Arnold's *Sohrab and Rustum*, l. 412.

327 **Port**: cf. Gray's *Bard*, l. 117

351. Fictitious· is here nearly equal to factitious or artificial

365. "The literature of the last century abounds with apostrophes to liberty That theme was the great commonplace of the time. Goldsmith has his laugh at it in the *Vicar of Wakefield*, Chap. XIX." (*Hales.*)

382–392. Chapter XIX of the *Vicar of Wakefield* furnishes a prose commentary on these lines. Less exception might be taken to the sentiments here expressed were Goldsmith's audience the same as that harangued by the excellent vicar.

388. Slaves: the allusion, probably, is to the "nabobs," that is, Englishmen who purchased boroughs at home with the immense wealth gained in India. "In this way one man is said to have made eight members of Parliament." (*Barrett.*)

397 The thought in the following passage reappears in the *Deserted Village*. l. 275 ff.

411 The sonorous sound of **Oswego** seems to have pleased Goldsmith's ear. Ct. *Threnodia Augustalis*, Part II l. 82.

412. The pronunciation of **Niagara** that is here required by the metre is still common in England. See Lippincott's *Gazetteer*.

420. This line was furnished by Johnson

429–434 Lines by Johnson.

431 Cf. *Paradise Lost*, I l. 254.

436 **Luke's iron crown**. in 1514 George and Luke Dosa headed a revolt in the Hungarian Republic The insurrection was quickly suppressed, and George, not Luke as Goldsmith says, was tortured with a red-hot iron crown for allowing himself to be proclaimed king. Boswell (*Life of Johnson*) gives the name of the brothers as Zeck, and one of Goldsmith's editors (Corney) fell into the mistake. See Forster's *Life of Goldsmith*, Vol. I. p. 370. **Damiens' bed of steel :** Robert François Damiens attempted to assassinate Louis XV. of France. The French in punishment inflicted tortures that rivalled the horrors of the Inquisition. Incisions were made in his arms and legs and boiling oil was poured in the wounds. Hot resin and molten lead were poured over his body, excoriated with red-hot pincers. Finally a horse was fastened to each leg and arm, and after an hour of agony the wretch was torn asunder. See Smollett's *History of England*, Vol. V. Chap. 3.

THE DESERTED VILLAGE.

The Deserted Village was published in 1770. Its success at the time was greater than that of *The Traveller* had been six years before. Posterity reads both with interest, but the later poem is the one by which Goldsmith is best known. In it he returns to some of the problems of the earlier poem, and makes his subject clearer by a contrast of varying conditions in the same nation. It furnishes particular instances by which the poet seeks to define what constitutes the real prosperity of a people. It is, however, a poetic effort, and any attempt to conform the poem to prosaic actualities of geography or political economy must destroy the splendor of the vivid images, fashioned though they are of material furnished by observation and memory. No imaginative production should be examined with over-scrupulous nicety for an identity with fact. In a search for trivialities the art of the master and the true beauty of his work must be overlooked. With this warning the supposed prototypes will be mentioned in the notes, in the hope that they may heighten the student's interest in the poem, without hampering that interest by the suggestion of fancies that, after all is said, are unessential conjectures. The poem was dedicated to Sir Joshua Reynolds, the great English painter, who returned the compliment by dedicating to Dr. Goldsmith the famous painting *Resignation*, "an attempt to express a character in *The Deserted Village*."

1. Sweet Auburn · Lissoy is supposed to be the original of Auburn. Dr. Strean, at one time curate of Kilkenny West and later of Athlone, made the most intelligent effort to identify the two. Lissoy is a parish in Kilkenny West, where Goldsmith's father moved when Oliver was two years old. Howitt says that "it [Lissoy] now consists of a few common cottages by the roadside, on a flat and by no means particularly interesting scene."

4. Parting: cf 1. 363; also Gray's *Elegy*, ll. 1 and 89.

12. Decent : the eighteenth-century use of this word, following its Latin derivation (*decens*), was equivalent to the modern 'becoming.' Cf. Pope, *Essay on Criticism*, l. 319.

17. Train : this is a favorite rhyme word with Goldsmith. It occurs seven times in this poem and twice in *The Traveller*, thus affording a reason for the charge that he, like Pope, has some pet expressions that are overworked.

23. Still : is used in a sense now obsolete, but usual in Shakespeare's day and common in the eighteenth century

27. Any school-boy will very willingly give a practical demonstration of the meaning of this verse to any one whose "ignorance is bliss." In Hawthorne's *Our Old Home*, read the chapter entitled "A London Suburb"

35. Lawn: here used in the sense of 'plain,' l. 1. See also Tennyson, *The Last Tournament*, l. 371. Cf. *The Traveller*, l. 319, and Gray's *Elegy*, l. 100.

44. In his *Animated Nature*, Goldsmith writes, "But of all these sounds [*i.e.* those made by geese, lapwings, jack-snipes, etc.] there is none so dismally hollow as the booming of the bittern." See *Isaiah*, xiv. 23, and xxxiv. 11.

52 Cf. *The Traveller*, l. 303 ff. See also *Vicar of Wakefield*, Chap. XIX.

53-54. This thought has found favor with many writers. See Bacon's essay *Of Great Place;* Burns's *Cotter's Saturday Night*, stanza XIX ; Thomson's *Summer*, l. 423 ff.

74. Manners : has rather the sense of customs. Cf. *Deserted Village*, l. 127 and note.

86. The same use of the pronoun **me** may be found in *The Traveller*, l. 32.

87. Husband out means to economize. The same figure occurs in *Macbeth*, Act. II. sc. i. l. 4.

101. Goldsmith has many repetitions of thought and phrase. Cf. note on l. 17. In *The Bee* he wrote, "By struggling with misfortunes, we are sure to receive some wound in the conflict: the only method to come off victorious is by running away."

111–112. Cf. the rhymes of ll. 95 and 96.

121. Cf. *Julius Cæsar*, Act. IV. sc. iii. l. 27.

124. In *Animated Nature* we find, "The nightingale's pausing song would be the proper epithet for this bird's music." Cf. note to l. 101. It is worth noting that the nightingale is not found in Ireland. The editor read in a newspaper not long since that "a nightingale had been caught in the vicinity of the Deserted Village and would be of more than passing interest to students of Goldsmith."

129. Investigators claim to have identified this woman with Catherine Geraghty.

142. Forty pounds seems to have been the average salary of a curate in the eighteenth century ; the "Vicar of Wakefield" received thirty-five pounds with certain perquisites. This description of the village preacher was written shortly after the poet learned of the death of his brother Henry. Read the introductory lines of *The Traveller* and compare with this passage. See also the comment on *The Deserted Village* in Irving's *Life of Goldsmith*. The use of **passing** in this line is Shakespearian. See *Othello*, Act. I. sc. iii. l 160, for a familiar line.

182. Steady zeal : in the first edition it was "ready zeal." Can you see any reason for the change ?

196. The village master : the picture that follows is supposed to be that of Goldsmith's early master Thomas (familiarly "Paddy") Byrne. In Irving's *Life of Goldsmith* may be found an interesting account of this eccentric pedagogue.

205–206. In Ireland, Scotland, and the provincial parts of England it is said the sound of 'l' is omitted in 'fault.' This may explain the imperfect rhyme. Cf. *Essay on Criticism*, ll. 170, 422

209. The **terms** were sessions of the universities and law courts. **Tides** are the times or sessions, particularly of the ecclesiastical year. But we still use noontide, eventide, etc.

210. To gauge : was to measure the capacity of casks. This was one of Burns's duties as excise commissioner. See *Standard Dictionary*.

232. The twelve good rules ascribed to King Charles I. are : 1. Urge no healths. 2. Profane no divine ordinances. 3. Touch no

K

state matters. 4. Reveal no secrets. 5. Pick no quarrels. 6. Make no companions. 7. Maintain no ill opinions. 8. Keep no bad company. 9. Encourage no vice. 10. Make no long meal 11. Repeat no grievances 12. Lay no wagers. **The royal game of goose**: was played by two persons, with dice and a board divided into sixty-two squares somewhat like the modern checker-board. On every fourth and fifth square a goose was painted, and if the player's dice fell on a goose, he might move on twice as many squares as the number thrown. Cf with this passage Goldsmith's *Description of an Author's Bedchamber*, the original draft of these lines It was part of a letter written to his brother Henry early in 1759

244. Woodman: used to mean a hunter.

248. Bliss· is another of the poet's favorite words. See *The Traveller*, ll. 58, 62, 82, 226, 267, 424. Cf. note on l. 17.

250 Cf. Ben Jonson's verses *To Celia*, and Scott's *Marmion*, canto V. stanza 12.

287. The use of **female** for woman, common as late as Scott's time and used *ad nauseam* by Cooper, is now considered a vulgarism.

288. Secure to please: means confident of pleasing. Cf with this construction that in l. 145.

316. Artist: in Goldsmith's time, was applied to any one engaged in the mechanic arts.

322 Chariots: is here used generically for carriages. **Torches**: used before the time of stationary street lights, were borne before carriages by servants called link-boys.

343 ff Goldsmith's notion of Georgia was no more hazy than that of many an Englishman of a later time The **Altama** is better known as the Altamaha.

368. Seats: is of course a classicism, here equivalent to 'homes.' Cf. Dryden's *Alexander's Feast*, l. 26 Note also the expressions, "seat of learning," "seat of government," "country seat," etc.

386. Things like these: "Not referring to anything in the context, but to the general subject of the poem, the innocence and happiness of country life." (Quoted by Rolfe.)

391 ff. Cf. *The Traveller*, l. 144.

398. Here begins an instance of the figure called vision. See *Macbeth*, Act. II. sc. i. l. 31 ff.

402. What distinction seems to be made between **shore** and **strand**?

418. The river Tornea or Torneo forms part of the boundary between Sweden and Russia, and flows into the Gulf of Bothnia.　Lake Tornea is in the northern part of Sweden.　**Pambamarca** is a mountain near Quito.

427–430. The last four lines of the poem were added by Dr. Johnson.　Goldsmith and Gray, in proportion to the amount written, have furnished more familiar quotations than any other English poets. Of the *Elegy* nearly every stanza contains some expression known wherever English is spoken.　Bartlett's *Familiar Quotations* includes seventy-four lines from *The Deserted Village*, and forty-six from *The Traveller*, besides numerous selections from Goldsmith's other poems.

Studies in English Composition.

By HARRIET C. KEELER, High School, Cleveland, Ohio, and EMMA C. DAVIS, Cleveland, Ohio. 12mo, cloth, 210 pages. Price, 80 cents.

THIS book is the outgrowth of experience in teaching composition, and the lessons which it contains have all borne the actual test of the class-room. Intended to meet the wants of those schools which have composition as a weekly exercise in their course of study, it contains an orderly succession of topics adapted to the age and development of high school pupils, together with such lessons in language and rhetoric as are of constant application in class exercises.

The authors believe that too much attention cannot be given to supplying young writers with good models, which not only indicate what is expected, and serve as an ideal toward which to work, but stimulate and encourage the learner in his first efforts. For this reason numerous examples of good writing have been given, and many more have been suggested.

The primal idea of the book is that the pupil learns to write by writing; and therefore that it is of more importance to get him to write than to prevent his making mistakes in writing. Consequently, the pupil is set to writing at the very outset; the idea of producing something is kept constantly uppermost, and the function of criticism is reserved until after something has been done which may be criticised.

J. W. Stearns, *Professor of Pedagogy, University of Wisconsin:* It strikes me that the author of your "Studies in English Composition" touches the gravest defect in school composition work when she writes in her preface: "One may as well expect a sea-anemone to show its beauty when grasped in the hand, as look for originality in a child, hampered by the conviction that every sentence he writes will be dislocated in order to be improved." In order to improve the beauty of the body we drive out the soul in our extreme formal criticisms of school compositions. She has made a book which teaches children to write by getting them to write often and freely; and if used with the spirit which has presided over the making of it, it will prove a most effective instrument for the reform of school composition work.

Albert G. Owen, *Superintendent, Afton, Iowa:* It is an excellent text. I am highly pleased with it. The best of the kind I have yet seen.

The Academy Series of English Classics.

THE works selected for this series are such as have gained a conspicuous and enduring place in literature; nothing is admitted either trivial in character or ephemeral in interest. Each volume is edited by a teacher of reputation, whose name is a guaranty of sound and judicious annotation. It is the aim of the Notes to furnish assistance only where it is absolutely needed, and, in general, to permit the author to be his own interpreter.

All the essays and speeches in the series (excepting Webster's Reply to Hayne) are printed without mutilation or abridgment. The Plays of Shakespeare are expurgated only where necessary for school use.

ADDISON.	De Coverley Papers. Edited by Samuel Thurber. Boards, 25 cents, cloth, 35 cents.
ARNOLD.	Essays in Criticism Edited by Susan S. Sheridan. Boards only, 20 cents.
BURKE.	Conciliation with the Colonies Edited by Professor C. B Bradley Boards, 20 cents, cloth, 30 cents
BURNS.	Selected Poems. Edited by Lois G. Hufford. Cloth only, 35 cents.
CARLYLE.	Edited by Henry W. Boynton. Essay on Burns. Boards only, 20 cents. Essay on Boswell's Johnson. Boards only, 20 cents.
ELIOT.	Silas Marner. Edited by W. Patterson Atkinson. Cloth only, 40 cents.
EMERSON.	Select Essays and Poems Edited by Eva March Tappan. Cloth only, 30 cents.
GOLDSMITH,	The Vicar of Wakefield Edited by R. Adelaide Witham. (*In preparation.*)
LOWELL.	The Vision of Sir Launfal. Edited by Dr. F. R. Lane. (*In preparation.*)
MACAULAY'S ESSAYS.	Edited by Samuel Thurber. Addison. Boards only, 20 cents. Chatham. Boards only, 20 cents. Clive. Boards only, 20 cents. Milton. Boards only, 20 cents. Milton and Addison (one vol.). Cloth only, 35 cts. Johnson. Boards only, 20 cents. Warren Hastings. Boards only, 20 cents.

The Academy Series of English Classics.

Continued.

MILTON.　　　Paradise Lost. Books I. and II. Edited by Henry
　　　　　　　W. Boynton. Boards, 20 cents; cloth, 30 cents.
　　　　　　　The Minor Poems. Edited by Samuel Thurber.
　　　　　　　(*In preparation.*)

POPE, GRAY, and GOLDSMITH.　Select Poems: An Essay on Criticism,
　　　　　　　Elegy, Progress of Poesy, The Traveller, and The
　　　　　　　Deserted Village. Edited by Geo. A. Watrous.
　　　　　　　(*At Press.*)

SHAKESPEARE.　Edited by Samuel Thurber.
　　　　　　　Julius Cæsar. Boards, 20 cents; cloth, 30 cents.
　　　　　　　Macbeth. Boards, 20 cents; cloth, 30 cents.
　　　　　　　Merchant of Venice. Boards, 20 cts.; cloth, 30 cts.
　　　　　　　As You Like It. Boards, 20 cents; cloth, 30 cents.
　　　　　　　Hamlet. Boards, 25 cents; cloth, 35 cents.

SYLE, L. D. (editor).　Four English Poems: Rape of the Lock, John
　　　　　　　Gilpin's Ride, The Prisoner of Chillon, and
　　　　　　　Rugby Chapel. Boards, 20 cents.

TENNYSON.　　Selections. Edited by Mary L. Avery. (*In prepa-
　　　　　　　ration.*)

THREE NARRATIVE POEMS. The Ancient Mariner, Sohrab and Rustum,
　　　　　　　and Enoch Arden. Edited by Geo. A. Watrous.
　　　　　　　Cloth only, 30 cents.

WEBSTER.　　Reply to Hayne. Edited by Professor C. B. Brad-
　　　　　　　ley. Boards only, 20 cents.

William Hand Browne, *Johns Hopkins University:* The text [of Burke's
Speech on Conciliation] is beautifully printed, and the notes, apparently, all that can be desired.

Felix E. Schelling, *University of Pennsylvania:* The book [Selections
from Emerson] seems to me thoroughly well done, as to selection, text,
and editing. The suggestive introduction, and the pertinency and brevity
of the notes, seem to offer an example in the doing of this sort of work.

The Critic, *Sept.* 9, 1896: The books of this series are well printed, and
seem to be in all respects the best of the very cheap editions of standard
literature.

Professor J. W. Stearns, *University of Wisconsin:* They [Conciliation
and Julius Cæsar] are very attractive books, handy, handsome, sub-
stantial, and well edited withal. It is very gratifying to see books in
every way so satisfactory and so cheap, issued for use in our schools.
The Series deserves to meet with general favor.

Composition-Rhetoric *for Use in Secondary Schools.*

By Professors F. N. SCOTT, of the University of Michigan, and J. V.
DENNEY, of Ohio State University. 12mo, cloth, 414 pages. Price,
$1.00.

IN the preparation of this work the authors have been guided
by three considerations.

First, it is desirable that a closer union than has hitherto
prevailed be brought about between secondary composition and
secondary rhetoric. The rhetoric which is found in this book is
meant to be the theory of the pupil's practice.

Second, it is desirable in secondary composition that greater
use be made of the paragraph than has hitherto been done. In
this book the paragraph is made the basis of a systematic method
of instruction.

A third idea which underlies the work is the idea of growth.
A composition is regarded not as a dead form, to be analyzed
into its component parts, but as a living product of an active,
creative mind.

In working out these ideas, care has been taken to provide
illustrative material of a kind that should be thought-provoking,
interesting, and valuable in itself, but not too far above the
standard of literary practice.

Professor Sophie C. Hart, *Wellesley College, Wellesley, Mass.:* As a whole
I consider it the best book on English Composition for the preparatory
school, and shall recommend it to all teachers who send students to
Wellesley.

Charles L. Hanson, *Mechanic Arts High School, Boston, Mass.* · I like the
book. Unlike many books, it does not appear unattractive. Unlike
others, it seems adapted to pupils of high school age. It ought to prove
inspiring. It must be suggestive both to pupil and to teacher.

Miss Harriet L Mason, *Drexel Institute, Philadelphia, Pa.* I find it all
that I could wish. The book fills a unique place in English text-books,
and is in the very van of the best teaching of composition. I shall use it
during the coming year.

Professor Robert Herrick, *University of Chicago* · It is really a long stride
in the right direction. It throws overboard much useless rubbish contained in the secondary school rhetoric, and teaches explicitly how to
get material, how to arrange it, and how to present it

Paragraph-Writing.

By Professor F. N. SCOTT, University of Michigan, and Professor J. V. DENNEY, Ohio State University. 12mo, 304 pages. Price, $1.00.

THE principles embodied in this work were developed and put in practice by its authors at the University of Michigan several years ago. Its aim is to make the paragraph the basis of a method of composition, and to present all the important facts of rhetoric in their application to it.

In Part I. the nature and laws of the paragraph are presented; the structure and function of the isolated paragraph are discussed, and considerable space is devoted to related paragraphs; that is, those which are combined into essays.

Part II. is a chapter on the theory of the paragraph intended for teachers and advanced students.

Part III. contains copious material for class work, selected paragraphs, suggestions to teachers, lists of subjects for compositions (about two thousand), and helpful references of many kinds.

The Revised Edition contains a chapter on the Rhetoric of the Paragraph, in which will be found applications of the paragraph-idea to the sentence, and to the constituent parts of the sentence, so far as these demand especial notice. The new material thus provided supplies, in the form of principles and illustrations, as much additional theory as the student of Elementary Rhetoric needs to master and apply, in order to improve the details of his paragraphs in unity, clearness, and force.

Professor J. M. Hart, *Cornell University:* The style of the writers is admirable for clearness and correctness. . . . They have produced an uncommonly sensible text-book. . . . For college work it will be hard to beat. I know of no other book at all comparable to it for freshman drill.

Professor Charles Mills Gayley, *University of California:* Paragraph-Writing is the best thing of its kind,—the only systematic and exhaustive effort to present a cardinal feature of rhetorical training to the educational world.

The Dial, *March,* 1894: Paragraph-Writing is one of the really practical books on English composition. . . . A book that successfully illustrates the three articles of the rhetorician's creed,—theory, example, and practice.

From Milton to Tennyson.

Masterpieces of English Poetry. Edited by L. DU PONT SYLE, University of California. 12mo, cloth, 480 pages. Price, $1.00.

IN this work the editor has endeavored to bring together within the compass of a moderate-sized volume as much narrative, descriptive, and lyric verse as a student may reasonably be required to read critically for entrance to college. From the nineteen poets represented, only such masterpieces have been selected as are within the range of the understanding and the sympathy of the high school student. Each masterpiece is given complete, except for pedagogical reasons in the cases of Thomson, Cowper, Byron, and Browning. Exigencies of space have compelled the editor reluctantly to omit Scott from this volume. The copyright laws, of course, exclude American poets from the scope of this work.

The following poets are represented : —

MILTON, by the L'Allegro, Il Penseroso, Lycidas, and a Selection from the Sonnets.
DRYDEN . . Epistle to Congreve, Alexander's Feast, Character of a Good Parson.
POPE . . . . Epistles to Mr. Jervas, to Lord Burlington, and to Augustus.
THOMSON . . Winter.
JOHNSON . . Vanity of Human Wishes.
GRAY . . . . Elegy Written in a Country Churchyard, and The Bard.
GOLDSMITH . Deserted Village.
COWPER . . Winter Morning's Walk.
BURNS . . . Cotter's Saturday Night, Tam O'Shanter, and a Selection from the Songs.
COLERIDGE . Ancient Mariner.
BYRON . . . Isles of Greece, and Selections from Childe Harold, Manfred, and the Hebrew Melodies.
KEATS . . . Eve of St. Agnes, Ode to a Nightingale, Sonnet on Chapman's Homer.
SHELLEY . . Euganean Hills, The Cloud, The Skylark, and the Two Sonnets on the Nile.
WORDSWORTH Laodamia, The Highland Girl, Tintern Abbey, The Cuckoo, The Ode to a Skylark, The Milton Sonnet, The Ode to Duty, and the Ode on the Intimations of Immortality.
MACAULAY . Horatius.
CLOUGH . . . Two Ships, the Prologue to the Mari Magno, and the Lawyer's First Tale.
ARNOLD . . The Scholar-Gypsy and the Forsaken Merman.
BROWNING . Transcript from Euripides (Balaustion's Adventure).
TENNYSON . Œnone, Morte D'Arthur, The Miller's Daughter, and a Selection from the Songs.

.

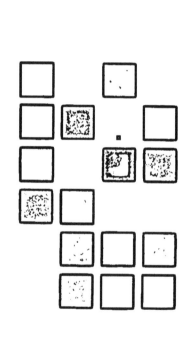

Lightning Source UK Ltd.
Milton Keynes UK
UKHW051716070621
385075UK00014B/282